CONNECT WITH COURAGE

PRACTICAL WAYS TO RELEASE FEAR AND FIND
JOY IN THE PLACES YOUR CHILDREN TAKE YOU

ROYA DEDEAUX, M.S., LMFT

Forever
CURIOUS
PRESS

ISBN: 978-1-989499-05-4 (ebook)
ISBN: 978-1-989499-06-1 (paperback)

Cover art by Aremy Stewart
Proofreading by Alice Romolo

John F. Nim's "Love Poem" from *Selected Poems by John F. Nims* copyright © 1982 by
University of Chicago Press, used with permission.

Published worldwide by Forever Curious Press
Erin, Ontario, Canada
forevercuriouspress.com

*This book should not replace appropriate mental health care, such as with a licensed
marriage and family therapist or psychiatrist. This book does not replace crisis emergency
services. This book is designed to provide a space to explore and process your feelings and
background. It is sold with the understanding that the author is not engaged to render any
type of psychological, legal, or any other kind of professional advice. The author shall not be
liable for any physical, psychological, emotional, financial, or commercial damages,
including, but not limited to, special, incidental, consequential or other damages. You are
responsible for your own choices, actions, and results.*

CONTENTS

SECTION V
Brainstorming

INTRODUCTION

This book is for you if:
You have kids
Your kids have interests

It is especially for you if:

- Some of those interests don't interest YOU.
- If you think they could be spending their time on something more worthwhile.
- You feel like there is some tension or distance between you and your children.
- You don't get why they want to spend all their time doing that thing.
- You love that they have something they love but feel out of touch and don't know how to connect with them about it.

Who Am I?

I'm a Licensed Marriage and Family Therapist with degrees in Counseling and Recreation and Leisure Studies. I have spent the bulk of my academic and professional career learning about how recreation, play, leisure, hobbies, interests, and passions impact—and are impacted by—mental health.

When I was eight years old, my Girl Scout troop did an exercise where we narrowed down a list of 377 values to our top three. Years later, I stumbled across the papers and filled them out again. I've done the same in the years since, maybe 15 times. Each time, the top two stay the same: creativity and curiosity.

When I was 20 years old, I took a wilderness expedition class at my university. We spent three weeks kayaking on Lake Powell, Utah. Twenty-four hours of that trip were spent in solitude. I sat on the red rocky side of that lake and wrote in my journal about why I was there, and why I thought following my interests was important. I wrote about why I thought people needed leisure time to be healthy. A few months later, I took that journal entry and used it as the basis for an essay titled, "This I Believe"—the last piece of required writing for my bachelor's program. I won the "This I Believe" scholarship from the department with my ideas about how recreation and leisure will change the world.

I teach three classes a semester to college students in the field of Recreation and Leisure Studies. They are high-level, experiential classes with a big focus on personal experience and having students share their thoughts and feelings. In an in-class exercise, I ask them to write a personal mission statement. Here is mine:

The Mission of Roya Dedeaux

To live committedly as wife, mother, therapist, and teacher. To use each role to the best of my ability to help people pursue their passions and increase their well-being as a result.

As a master's student, I discovered the field of narrative therapy and found an immediate understanding and vocabulary for many of my beliefs. I found the language for what happens when we internalize negative thoughts about ourselves and the powerful changes and healing that can happen when we add to our story.

Narrative theory requires that we accept who we are, how we came to be, and allow ourselves to add richness to the story. When applied to the parenting work I do with clients, it is about accepting that you may not have had the best parents. You may have internalized beliefs about your skills or qualifications that get in your way. You might come from a fear-based place, which gets in the way of seeing your children for who they are. Narrative theory says to understand and name those things, externalize them, then add to them. They are part of you, not the whole of you. My philosophy is shaped by narrative theory, as is this book. It is here to help you add to the story of you.

For many years at an annual conference, I orchestrated a family-centered space called "Fiberland." It was an open studio for families to come and learn and spend open-ended time playing with yarn, crocheting, knitting, and exploring other fiber arts. I watched relationships between siblings, parents, grandparents, and kids through the lens of this particular interest area. I was able to provide a space and be a witness to hundreds of parents supporting their kids in this interest. As a therapist, I often see relationship damage done— hearts broken; communication and connection failing. But during the weekend each year I spent in Fiberland, I saw the opposite. I saw parents leaning in close to listen to their children, kids beaming while they held up their felted creation to show their moms, dads re-threading needles for their sons, and siblings finding the right color yarn for their brothers and sisters. It is more than a powerful metaphor to say that this connection was happening with yarn; that the people who walked in felt close-knit and tied together. There is something tangibly powerful when you walk into a room of happily productive people who are interested in each other and what they are creating.

I share my stories to give you a taste of how my philosophy developed. Looking back, I see a very direct path. Over and over again, I've seen the connection between a child having their interests valued by the adults around them and their well-being. I have gathered more stories and added richness to the concepts. I have honed some of the language, but what has changed the most is the scope of my vision. I now see how this small kernel of an idea can be broadened and generalized, with the potential to substantially impact many lives. It turns out that my sun-soaked thoughts about how positive leisure experiences are necessary for an individual's well-being were only the first rung on a very tall ladder. If we continue to climb, we can reach our families, our broader relationships, and society as a whole.

I believe that protecting children's interests is a crucial first step to finding global solutions to global problems. I also believe that every child's experience is, in itself, important enough to warrant an entire book. I'm glad you're here.

Why did I write this book?

I wrote this book because the vast majority of clients I see have some damaging self-talk about how they or their children spend their leisure time that directly impacts their sense of self and that of their children. In the field of psychology, there is a concept known as the "multi-generational transmission process." This is a long name for the idea that some things continue to impact a family, even generations later. Your attitudes regarding play, leisure time, work ethic, and parenting come from somewhere, and that somewhere was impacted by your parent's parenting, their parent's parenting, which in turn were impacted by natural disasters, wars, trauma, and events big and small. Not all that we pass down is unhealthy, but it certainly is always healthier when we are conscious and aware of how our internalized messages and values are shaping our decision-making and our children's lives.

Many of the messages passed down through generations have to do with play, leisure, free time, or recreational activities. I truly believe that one of the best things we can do for the mental and emotional health of our children is to actively honor their interests. Yet, sometimes we lack the creativity or imagination to do that well or to find solutions for logistical problems.

The goal of this book is to help you address a few areas:

1. Logistical barriers (things like money, space, time)
2. Emotional barriers (things like your messaging about the value of play or work, fears about type of play, distaste for content)

This book is designed to be a starting place to think about these topics.

So, let's get started! You've got this book, you've got a pen, you've got your coffee, and you've got Netflix going with something that won't stop in just a few minutes? It's okay if your kids are around; you don't need perfect silence and concentration. (And be realistic, are you going to get that anyway? Don't wait for perfect situations before attempting to do better. That's a technique our monkey minds use to keep the status quo and avoid making changes.) Some of these activities will be better if you have your actual, real-life kids right there in front of you for prompting anyway.

I like to think of this book as being deceptively simple. The formatting is minimalistic. The text is plain. I want this to feel safe and unassuming. If you are having any feelings of intimidation, take a minute to take some deep breaths and remember that I'm on your side. I want you to open this book up and feel like you've landed somewhere safe and comforting and helpful. I am beaming encouraging thoughts in your direction. I like you, and I really like your kid. No matter where you are, that is our starting point, and this book will only improve what you've got going on. I am assuming the best of you and your intentions and your love for your children. The book is simple, but the places it will lead you will be complex, deep, and steeped in past messaging and—dare I say it?—baggage.

I am a therapist. And as a therapist, I see myself as a sort of guide and mirror for my clients. There is an order to things in a therapy session. We start, often with something that seems trivial ("What did you do this week?") and then connect stories until we discover meaningful themes. We dive in and explore the deep end, while I reflect patterns back at my clients. It is often uncomfortable and painful, and then, together, we work our way back out of that to a place of calm or acceptance or moving forward. I see it like a story arc in a television show—each individual session (or episode) has an arc, and so does the whole season. This book isn't any different. To create that arc, I recommend starting with section one and moving through why this is a vital topic to explore, then on to what happens when things go wrong (and when things go right), and then onto the how: working through the tools and exercises in order to address the barriers that may be in your way. I have organized the book to have a specific progression that involves a balance between emotional and logistical topics and themes. It is like a portable therapy session that you get to open and work on whenever you can.

I don't imagine any parent has the time, space, or emotional capacity to work through this book in one sitting, so don't put that sort of pressure on yourself. Work through it in order the first time, imagining that completing an exercise unlocks the next. However, once an exercise is unlocked, I encourage you to go back and reflect on prior exercises as much as you can. You'll think of more to add to them or other ways they connect to your kids' lives.

As you read, have a notebook sitting beside you. Get a silly one that costs less than a dollar so you don't feel too precious about it. Don't worry about your grammar or your handwriting. Just write as prompted and wherever your thoughts take you. Don't edit yourself, unless I ask you to in the exercise. Most of this book requires brainstorming and exploring. Doodle between your words. Foster connections between random thoughts. Add sticky notes to your notebook. If something reminds you of what you wrote on a previous page, go back and add more. There's space. It's yours. You're also welcome to download and print a PDF workbook that includes all the exercises at www.royadedeaux.com/courage.

Throughout the book, I have included statements from parents I have seen making their relationship with their children the priority, and who I think have something of immense value to share. They are real people, with real kids, who have real interests that they actively support. They are not clients of mine—any stories I share throughout this book that refer to my clients have been changed to honor the ethical and legal obligations of confidentiality.

One last thing—this book is not a mind-reader. Some of the questions might not exactly apply to your specific situation. Generalize if you need to. Skip a question if you need to. Better yet, replace that question with another. Be honest with yourself—if you skip, maybe that's part of the problem? If you are working through this book, chances are there are things you are currently doing or ways you are thinking that are not working as well as you would like for you or your children. Let this book challenge your mental status quo. The more you put into it, the more you will get out of it.

SECTION I

OUR BRAINS AND OUR HEARTS

WHY THIS IS OF VITAL IMPORTANCE

In my years of working with families, I have listened to their stories, helped them work through their struggles, and been alongside as they discovered important themes. Without realizing it, I started to gather their moments and watched patterns emerge in front of me. Big-picture patterns that started to change the shape of how I viewed relationships, family dynamics, and even mental health and well-being. I helped individuals and families while seeing how each new situation started to fit within a theme that was emerging. I recognize now that I was conducting my own qualitative research on families, mental health, fear, and supporting (or not) a child's interests.

What has emerged turned into this book—a foray into the most important common themes I collected. I believe this topic is vast and vital to our personal happiness, to our relationship satisfaction, and even has implications for our societal and global well-being. While I see this far-reaching connection, I want you to focus in: think about your actual real children, your life, and your small moments. You are the subject matter of this book.

∾

The Mental Health Connection

Here's a story I have heard a lot from my clients:

"I have anxiety or depression or both. I don't trust my feelings, I have difficulty making decisions, I worry about the outcome of my actions, I am scared to express myself or voice my thoughts, I am scared that I won't say or do the right thing, and that I will make others upset with me."

An incredibly common factor among my clients? They don't trust themselves because their parents didn't trust them. One arena in which this is illustrated over and over and over again? Play, games, recreation, and leisure.

I had a client whose parent brought them to me because of depression and lack of confidence. Once I met with them, they confessed to deeper depression than their parent knew about— suicidal ideation and overall feelings of low self-worth. They spoke quietly, eyes down, and did not want to share very much with me. I cast about for rapport-building questions and finally asked about their TV watching habits. I saw a little flicker of interest, and I asked some follow-up questions. A few minutes later, it was like an entirely different person had walked into the room. As it turns out, they were passionate about one specific television show, to the point of becoming a leading expert on social media. They had a website, an online community, and spent hours every day discussing and processing the universe created by this show. This interest had branched out to other interests, created opportunities for friendships, and built the foundation for technical skills that are useful by anyone's measure of success.

When I asked if their parent knew all of this, the light went back out of their eyes. The answer was no; their parent had no idea they had this rich, amazing world based on a TV show. In fact, their parent often spoke disparagingly about this show, severely limited their online time, used limiting access as a threat, and used harsh language when describing the activity to others. This led to their child feeling all sorts of terrible things about themselves, and very much damaged the relationship between them.

It is not a difficult connection to make: I have Interest. If Parent thinks Interest is Bad, then I must be Bad for having Interest.

NOT EVERY PARENT/CHILD relationship is as extreme an example as the one I wrote about, but some level of this negativity exists in an incredibly high number of relationships. (By the way, this is a book geared towards parents and their children, but the same principles apply to relationships with your peers, other family members, or significant other.) It is easy for even the most well-intended parent to inadvertently put down their child's interest, even if no harsh words are spoken.

I enjoy both knitting and crocheting. Although my husband has never done either, it is a piece of goodwill and connection when he asks me correctly how my crocheting is going. When he wants to be funny and get under my skin, he says, despite seeing crochet hook in hand, "How's your sewing?" If it weren't a long-standing joke in our relationship, it would be a dismissive thing to say. It would show a lack of understanding or caring to understand. It's a short and relatively painless interaction, from his point of view, but it could be enough—especially if this attitude is pervasive through other interactions—to cause a barrier between us. It communicates that, to him, this interest isn't worth even naming correctly, which means it isn't worth caring about, which means the person doing it (me) isn't worth caring about.

That might not seem like a logical sequence to some parents who know they love their children even if they don't love their interests. But these messages can seep into our children's consciousness. They make us feel a certain way—disregarded, small, isolated—and those feelings tend to stick. It isn't always logical. There are other factors, like your history, your resiliency, and your personal narrative. But, over and over again, I have seen support for their interests be a vital piece of a person's mental health and relationships—both as a cause for when it doesn't feel healthy and as a place where healing can happen.

The other extreme is also true. People with high levels of self-esteem, self-efficacy, and self-worth, show a history of taking themselves and their wants seriously. This has usually been modeled to them by their parents. They have parents who show an interest in their interests, use respectful and admiring language, pay attention, and actively support their kids as they pursue their passions.

The First Exercise!

How would you describe how your kid spends their day? Write about the activities they choose to do as well as their scheduled activities. Put in as much detail as you can.

[Whenever I ask you to write, grab your journal and remember that you don't need to share this with anybody so don't worry about spelling mistakes or grammatical errors. Don't censor or edit yourself as you write. During the initial writing phase, just keep your hand moving and don't spend too much time criticizing yourself. There's no wrong. Just answer the question. We'll explore it after.]

Okay, let's go through it. Re-read what you wrote.

What do you notice?

Go through and circle any part of what you wrote that feels especially emotional to you, no matter what the emotion.

List the words or phrases you circled.

If you had to pick one word that summarizes how you feel about what you just wrote, what is it?

Now, pay attention to your language use—did you use any of the following words or phrases?

"Addiction"

"Obsession/Obsessed"

"Literally all the time"

"Won't stop"

"More than they should"

"Unsafe amount"

"Never wants to stop"

"Spends all day if I let them"

"Ridiculous"

"I don't get it"

"Too much"

"Not enough"

The language we use matters. It reinforces biases and ideas. It communicates and solidifies feelings. It matters if you said your kid is "addicted" to something. It doesn't mean you are a terrible person for thinking or writing it, but it does say that you feel negatively about their interest. It also communicates that you are coming from a place of fear. None of the words or phrases above have particularly good connotations associated with them, especially when used to describe how a kid chooses to spend their time.

How would you feel if you overheard someone you love (like your significant other) talking about your interests this way?

Cross out every time you use one of those negative words or phrases in your initial paragraph and come up with a replacement. How can you reframe it? Here are some ideas for new words, and try to come up with some of your own.

Interested

Passionate

In-depth

Pursuit

Dedicated

Concentration

Love

Focused

Fascinated

Engaged

_____

_____

_____

Write a new version of the statement we started with describing how your kid spends their day, using your new positive and more respectful language.

More about Language Use

Avoid generalizing.

Don't say, "watching TV" or "on a screen" or "playing a game." What TV shows? What genre? What season? What episodes? Do you know what draws them in? Have they seen this before, or is it new? Pay attention over time and notice all the different things they might do —maybe different shows, or movies and TV, or video-chatting with a friend, or looking up instructions, or playing a game, or watching a YouTube video, or...

Be specific.

If you are going to talk to them about their interest, make sure you use the right vocabulary. Use your knowledge to show you're paying attention to the details. This translates into feelings of being cared for and seen.

Be realistic.
Do you say things like, "all day" "literally alllll the time"? That tells me that you are catastrophizing and operating from fear, fear, fear.

HONORING YOUR CHILD'S INTERESTS

In my university class, "Universality of Play," I recently asked my 35 students if their parents valued play. They were fairly quiet. A few nodded slowly, some opened their eyes wide and shook their head no. I followed up with, "Those of you who said yes, your parents valued your play, how did you know? Did they walk up to you and look in your eyes and say, 'Son! I value your play!' or were there other methods of communication?" Then the hands went up.

They knew their parents valued play when...

They would pay for activities, equipment, and supplies.

They would drive to their events, stay to watch, and participate in the "extra" activities (like slicing oranges and bringing snacks).

They would pay for the new versions of old games/equipment/supplies.

They would know the other teammates names, the coaches, or know about the small-group politics/social drama that was happening.

They would dedicate a space to it at home, like put up a goal or a net, or have a table ready to paint at.

They would tell relatives or friends about their child's most recent activity, accomplishment, or experience in a proud, "show off" way.

When I asked students how they knew their play wasn't valued, it was essentially the opposite. Their parents did not pay attention to the intricacies of their interests, did not spend money on supplies or equipment, would not drive or facilitate, and would speak in harsh or demeaning ways about their activities. Or, their interest was simply discounted as not being worth air, space, or energy.

Time. Money. Resources. Attitude.

Our decisions about how we use these things communicate a lot to our children. My students were very clear that they understand now how their parents did not always have an abundance of money or time to spend on their soccer, hockey, dance, etc., but when they had an attitude of support, their kids felt it.

I can't speak enough about the importance of honoring your child's interests, **no matter what they are.**

At the same time, I want to acknowledge the fact that it can sometimes be difficult for parents to do. I have seen that parents who are feeling threatened or under-supported themselves are least likely to be able to think expansively and creatively. So, consider this a plug for getting extra support. Maybe that looks like getting coffee with a friend, posting in an online support group, or getting therapy (get therapy), but you need to recharge your resources to be your best self. As you go through this book, remember to think, speak, and write kindly about yourself, even while you are analyzing, exploring, and attempting to do better. Both things are possible.

Someone once asked me if I thought I had gaps in my knowledge. I remember being so surprised by this question—the answer was so immediate and so obvious. Yes! Of course, I have gaps in my knowledge! Not only do I have gaps in my knowledge, it is *more* gap than knowledge! If you think about the information that I have in my head compared to *all the information in the world*, the fraction is so small I don't even know if it's computable (speaking of gaps in my knowledge). I do not know everything. I do not know most things. I do not even know many things, when you look at it that way. Although schools provide standards for students to meet in each grade, all you need to do is teach one semester of university courses to realize that most people do not retain the majority of the information they were provided in school. We learn many lessons in our childhood and teenage years, but the things that tend to stick with us are not factual pieces of information. So, given that we will not have perfect recall of all factual information, I am suggesting that, from a mental health perspective, it is far more valuable to spend time helping people learn *how* they learn.

We know a few things about the way the mind (and children) work. We know that we do not retain information when we are resistant to hearing it. We know that when things are fun, feel like a game, or are interest-driven, we retain more. Have you ever watched a child who can't remember the steps of a simple math problem, remember long and complicated video game cheat codes? You've seen this in action.

Stop trying to make them learn things they don't want to.

Instead, use their interests as the vehicle for learning *how* they learn.

Yes, they will forget specific information. They will forget average rainfalls and algebraic equations and the plot of *The Three Musketeers*. The specifics will fall away over time, like needles off a pine tree. The core memories left will be based in emotion. They will remember the anxiety of not feeling good at the math problems, or the stress of trying to finish a book report, or the resentment towards their parent for putting them in that situation—the internalized, "I'm not good enough."

Or, they might remember the joy of learning something cool about their favorite subject. The fun of connecting with their parent over what feels like a game. The glow of satisfaction at being able to teach their mom or dad a thing or two about a subject they are an expert in. The positive feelings of mastery, curiosity, and engagement.

These are the things we remember. The things that become the core of us.

"I'll never forget the day I sat worrying about my 15-year-old son who spent all his time (years, really) creating nerf gun weaponry and strange gadgets. "What would he possibly do with *that* when he grew up?" I wondered. How could that be useful? And then I hit upon an idea. He needed a theater arts department! He and I found a props design class at our local community college and we signed him up for the upcoming semester. The first night of class he texted me, "I love this so much. This is what I want to do with my life!" Nine years later he has held true to that dream. He finished at the community college with a certificate in stage management five years ago and has been stage managing ever since! Today he is the stage manager for a Cafeteria Kids children's theater company, Napa Valley Shakespeare Festival and Napa Valley College. He's happy, fulfilled and gets paid for his work!"

— Susie

I LIKE to think of the way our brain works as walking through a field. If you walk the same path over and over again, in time, the earth becomes compacted. You create a walkway, and you probably keep walking that path because it's the easiest one to take. Similarly, our brains often take the easy, most-used route. Our brains go through something called "neural pruning" throughout childhood, essentially pruning away underused neurons and synapses. The neural pathways that get used the most stay. The chemicals that help make those connections are called neurotransmitters, and the way we perceive those chemicals are our emotions. If we experience a childhood where we walk the path of anxiety over and over again, it makes it that much easier to tap into anxiety. If we experience satisfaction or curiosity regularly, we trend in that direction. The neurotransmitters we experience often become the default.

This is a gross oversimplification of a complex and fascinating field, but the end result is that our jobs as parents and educators really ought to be to help prepare the brains of children for the most resilient outcome we can. And that direction is full of play and hands-on learning. We ought to be facilitating our children's engagement with their interests and eliminating situations and environments that routinely cause internalized levels of despair or feelings of 'not-good-enough.' This doesn't mean eliminating all opportunities for stress or struggle because learning that we can get through those difficulties is important too, which I will discuss at greater length later in this book. It does mean we can take a good, long look at how often we are providing opportunities for better neural development and learning, and how often we are standing in the way of that.

When our core is full of satisfaction, contentment, joy, and curiosity, we soak up new learning like a sponge. We aren't resistant to it—there aren't walls built up to protect us from stressful situations. Brains work by making connections. When we support our children's interests, we open up so many connections for them as well. That is good for brain development! And, as far as our neurotransmitters go, we are also more open and receptive and joyful! We have confidence in our skills, higher levels of self-esteem, and higher levels of self-efficacy.

Self-efficacy is important and interesting. It has to do with our sense of being able to figure things out for ourselves; of being competent. It is our sense of being able to take on challenges. It is this sense that is heightened when parents protect their children's passions. That helps a person walk more confidently into uncertain situations, knowing that even if they don't have the answers, they can figure it out. It is a critical factor in building resilience, which is an important counter-trait to depression, anxiety, and being impacted by trauma or grief.

Self-efficacy, as it turns out, is increased or decreased depending on the relationship children have with their parents or other influential adults in their life. It is related to the amount of shame versus support they received in different developmental stages. Kids with better relationships with parents—whose parents are engaged, supportive, and interested in their passions and opinions—build a foundation for optimal self-efficacy and resiliency.

If you read the section about neural pruning and thought, "Well, my childhood was terrible so I'm a lost cause!" have no fear. Our brains also have "plasticity"—we can heal. And the place where healing can be the most effective? In play and recreation. I have had many parents tell me that their focus on supporting their children and in parenting differently than they were parented had surprising self-healing results. They were doing this for their kids and ended up reaping many personal benefits. This type of restorative parenting is a wonderful, natural outcome of better relationships.

Use your children's interests as a platform to connect and build better relationships with them.

If you can eliminate a sense of pressure and coercion, it opens you up to be on their team, rather than be their adversary. Every time your kid says, "Hey, parent! Look at this neat thing!" and you stop what you are doing to look, you are connecting. Every time you say, "Hey, child! What is that neat thing?" and you pay attention to their answer, you are connecting. These connections are important. They create the secure attachments that humans need to form a healthy sense of self, to increase self-efficacy and self-worth, and to have healthy relationships in the future.

That self-worth is important, especially when we think about what kinds of tricky, questionable, or scary situations our kids might face in their future. When I think about what I want for my children in their lives and future relationships, I want them to trust themselves. To be able to look at a situation and trust their gut feeling about safety and comfort. To trust their sense of right and wrong. To trust their abilities and skills. To trust themselves to be assertive. I want them to trust their voice, to take up space in the world, to adapt without losing themselves, to work in a team, and to be a leader.

I want them to trust themselves.

I don't want them to lose themselves to other, stronger voices, to pressure, coercion, or group-think.

We learn how to make big, important decisions through practice. Over and over again we impart messages. Over and over again we help our kids learn to trust their own voice—or not.

We first learn to trust ourselves with our parents, and it's never through conversation. It doesn't go like this:

Parent: "I trust you, my child."
Child: "Okay, rad."

It doesn't look like that. The opportunities happen often, and usually through choices about how we spend time and our actions.

This is a very common scenario:

Child: Playing computer game.
Parent: "It's time to get off now."
Child: "I don't wanna."
Parent: "You have to."
Child: "Okay, just 5 more minutes."
Parent: "NOW."

I know, as parents, we are thinking bigger picture. We are thinking, *they've already been on the computer for a long time and we need them to go empty the dishwasher because we have to load the dishwasher and if we don't do that now then we don't eat dinner at a reasonable hour and if we don't eat dinner at a reasonable hour no one goes to bed and then we are all cranky and tomorrow we have this really big, fun thing coming up and so it's really important and something you'll enjoy if only you would get off the computer NOW—it's for your own good, darn it!*

Or, we're thinking about the vastness of the whole big world, and we've decided that they could use some non-computer time. Either way, we do have wisdom and experience that our children do not.

If only that's what they were actually hearing when we said that. Because, in that same "NOW" scenario, what message does the kid probably hear?

I have a timeline and I think it's important and I'm ignoring the fact that you finally just got to the level you have been working for and I'm ignoring the fact that your friend just got online and I'm ignoring the plans you had made and the atmosphere you've created and the things that are important to you and the fact that you developmentally cannot care more about tomorrow's hypothetical fun situation than the right-now that you are engrossed in. I care about what I want. I don't care as much about you.

Okay, so, they might also know you love them and care about them and intellectually understand that it's not as binary as "care about me" or "care about you," but there is the message that your wants (even if they are wise and valuable) are more important than how they are choosing to spend their time. You are imposing your values onto theirs. There is no getting around that.

Exercise 2

Take a moment and write down a common conflict-laden scenario between you and your child.

What is the environment like when this scene usually happens?

What gives this scene its emotional charge? Are there outside pressures? Internal ones?

What are some of the words you would use to describe the scenario between you?

Conflict. Stress. Pressure. Anger. Resentment. Battle. These are all words that, as a therapist, I've heard parents and children use to describe this situation. They are not fun words. They are not happy, relationship-building words! They are words of war and strife!

How would you like those interactions to go? Describe what would feel like success in that moment.

When children see that their parent trusts them with decisions, especially about how and what to spend their time on, it imparts a poignant lesson—actions speak much louder than words.

What happens when the scenario goes like this?

Child: Spends time playing computer game.
Parent: Lets them.

Giving your child the gift of choice and time? Those are powerful gifts.

I want to take it one step further.

What if:

Child: Spends time playing computer game.
Parent: Cuts up an apple and brings it to them at the computer, sits for a while and watches, gives them a kiss on the top of their head, smiles at how involved their kid is and how much joy they are getting from it, takes a picture to send to their spouse with a loving caption, does a little bit of research to find the new cool game/exhibit/sound-track/whatever that connects to their game.
Child, later that day: Asks to show their parent their newest character skin, describes in animated detail the latest battle/map/building, is open and excited and willingly connects with their parent on this topic, which inevitably leads to other topics.

CULTIVATING CONNECTION

That's the dream. That's the game-changer. That type of scenario, playing out many times, over time, are like individual knit stitches in a large blanket. A blanket where you and your kid get to sit together, connected, warm and fuzzy, safe and secure. It makes an impression—a lasting one. When your kid is no longer right there next to you, that foundation of trust carries them into the rest of the world.

Maybe that last scenario is one you have dreamed of enacting, ready and willing with time, apple slices, and Pinterest. Alas, you have a different despair, "But my kid isn't interested in anything!"

You might have picked up this book with a little bit of a sinking heart and wishful thinking. You might be thinking to yourself, "I WISH I could connect with my children through their interests, but they aren't interested in ANYTHING!"

I have heard this story many times, from many worried parents, whose pent up good intentions act like bouncing springs inside of them. These parents feel like they are underutilized, like their amazing creativity and desire to truly support and connect with their children is being wasted.

"They don't do ... anything?" I ask. "If you let them do what they want to do, do they stare at a wall? For how many hours in a row?"

"Well ... no ... not exactly," the well-intended parent usually says, slightly hesitantly. "I mean, I make them go to piano/do their homework/read a chapter/go to soccer, but then all they want to do is play some video game/watch some YouTube video. They'd do THAT for hours and hours if I let them! That's what I mean! They wouldn't choose anything valuable!"

"Ah," I say, understanding better now. "So, you've got an idea of things you want them to be interested in, but they are choosing to do something else."

That is a very different scenario than what the parents initially presented to me. This is a situation in which their children are actively—through their actions and choices and behaviors—showing their parents what their interests are, and the parents are deciding that they aren't valuable *enough* to make the list of activities they are willing to support.

For many parents, it's because they have a vision of their family gathered around a table, laughing, playing a board game, and eating homemade organic kale chips, while a soft glow of light emanates from no particular source. Other parents dreamed that their children's initial interest in taking baths with rubber duckies would lead to trips to museums and aquariums and tide pools, foreshadowing an astounding marine biology career. I don't mean to minimize. These are beautiful dreams. I have them too, and many more like them. The thing is though, that those dreams are getting in our way.

Whatever your dream was, if your children's interests don't a) look like what you had planned, or b) seem to have much room for connecting with you, it can be really hard to realize that what your children are choosing to do when they aren't being forced to do other things *is* what they are interested in.

It's your job, as the parent and adult, to find the value in what they are choosing to do. Not the other way around. Saying, "I want to connect with my kids," and then handing them a list of parent-approved interests to choose from is limiting and disingenuous. Parenting isn't going to meet your expectations in many ways. Your kids aren't going to meet your expectations in many ways. This can be disappointing, but it can also be surprising and wonderful, beyond your wildest imagination—if you are open to it. But you need to let it take its own shape. You have to realize that your dreams, while beautiful, were made without knowing your actual, real kid. And that real kid of yours is a real human being. They get to make decisions and to have interests, desires, and values that are separate from yours.

You can, however, join them. Most kids I have encountered *want* their parents to join them. We want our parents' approval and connection, even after years of neglect or abuse. If yours are acting like they don't, it could be a defense mechanism. Maybe they are trying to protect something they love from being put down. Maybe they tried to reach out to you before and you used some degrading language that didn't feel good. Maybe they don't think you would understand. Maybe you have been too heavy-handed—when they gave you a drop of what they were interested in, you took the reins and tried to make it their whole world, imposing your values about *how* to be interested in something.

Exercise 3

If this might be the case, ask yourself ...

Why is this thing not valuable to you?

What are you worried might happen if you let them play longer?

Have you ever watched something silly and enjoyed it?

Have you sat down and looked at this from their perspective?

What does their body language say about their passion? Are they invested? Engrossed? Focused?

If what you wrote rings negative, try reframing it now.

THE VALUE OF PLAY

Above all else, I believe that your relationship with your children is going to be the thing that helps you all through any rough time ahead. I believe that there is no piece of factual information as important as children keeping their curiosity and playfulness intact. I believe this is fundamental in their ability to problem solve, thrive through struggle, have healthy relationships, and be successful as adults.

I know that every adult who chose to pick this book up did so out of love for their kid. If you didn't care, you would not be trying to do better. So often our fears get in our way. Watching our children do anything that feels like excess taps into our fears of addiction and substance abuse. We are getting bombarded with pop psychology and bad science related to video game addiction, tapping directly into our fears of what happens if we let them play games for more than eight minutes a day. If we watch them stay still for too long, or opt-out of family tasks, we worry it's indicative of laziness and that it won't be very long before they have lost their only possible job, are using substances, and are unable to survive without us. We put limits and restrictions on the things they are showing us they love because we are afraid that, without adult-imposed moderation, they will never be able to get up in time to get to work or their college classes.

We have to let them be kids before we worry that much about their adulthood.

We have to let them learn things later in life, not all at once as children.

We have to remember that we can learn quickly to behave as required when there is a need—when they want that paycheck, they will get up for that paycheck. It does not take eight years to learn that.

We have to remember what research actually shows us about addiction and turning to substances. We now understand that the thing that drives many people to use substances is a feeling of being disengaged and disconnected. When our regular life is not engaging, when we do not feel like our life or we matter, and when we don't have fulfilling and intrinsically satisfying work to do, we turn to *something* to help us escape the discomfort we feel in our own skin. This is the breeding ground for alcoholism, for addiction. Children who are involved and invested in their passions are much less likely to feel this way.

Engagement with interests and feeling connected to something bigger than themselves—a bigger, epic universe—is the antidote to drug use. Kids who have had their interests supported and have been able to dive in and form connections with people of various ages and backgrounds based on their common interest, who have been able to see people who are better or more knowledgeable and develop aspirations and goals, are much less likely to look for a way to feel differently. There is less need for self-medication or escapism. They are less likely to use drugs.

Nothing that I know of brings people together to share in epic goal achievements better than video games do. Those hours of playing do not indicate potential addiction. They are the opposite. They are the antidote.

Sometimes self-medication in the form of substance abuse or dependence has its catalyst with feeling unable to cope with the stressors of life, clinical depression, or anxiety. One of my favorite quotes is by Brian Sutton, "The opposite of play is not work—the opposite of play is depression." Increased playfulness is helpful at any point on the spectrum, for any mental health diagnosis.

Take a typical, levels-based video game, for example. When you take that controller in your hands, you immediately agree to the following: *I am going to try. I might fail. I probably will fail. And I will try anyway. I will use the tools I have available to me. I will use resources and allies in the game. I will engage with the goals and mission of this game. I am capable of trying, probably becoming better able to do the next step of this game, and potentially winning.*

I can't think of anything better for our mental health than repeated practice thinking those things. There is optimism: "Maybe I will win!" There is resiliency: "If I fail, I will try again!" There is creativity: "Here is another solution I can try!" There is teamwork: "I can play with people/ask somebody/look online!" There is a feeling of being connected to a purpose and accomplishing small goals to reach a bigger one. These are fundamentally important qualities to practice and traits to possess.

Being able to look at a challenge and feel like you have the skills to handle it is one of the most important tools for dealing with anxiety, depression—or life. When we are faced with a challenge, we tell ourselves a story. Maybe it's the story of how we are a victim to circumstance and are unable to meet the challenge. Or, we can tell ourselves the story of how we can take on the challenge. It doesn't mean there isn't a challenge—but the story we tell ourselves about how *we* face the challenge matters. What we internalize matters.

Parents, trust your children's interests. Being engaged in something not only has benefits, it also helps them wire their brains to trust themselves, to be open to resources and creativity, and to be resilient in the face of challenge.

One of the important things we learn when we use play and interests as the foundation for our children's days is that there are a lot of different ways to learn! It is just straight-up false that we learn best when reading from a book while sitting at a table in a room full of 30 people the same age we are. There is not one teeny little ounce of research that proves that sitting inside a classroom doing worksheets or listening to a person talk about a subject is how we learn best. Our society is set up to value a certain type of learner, and a certain kind of intelligence, but it is up to us to remember and show that we value the whole awesome variety.

When your kid engages in play, that is an opportunity for you to look for strengths they might not show when sitting at a classroom desk. When your kid pursues their interests, those are detectable clues for you to gather about your child's intelligence type.

Howard Gardner famously wrote about the eight intelligences he believed to be present in humanity. He submitted that people have linguistic intelligence, logical-mathematical intelligence, spatial intelligence, bodily-kinesthetic intelligence, musical intelligence, interpersonal intelligence, intrapersonal intelligence, and natural intelligence. The first few are lauded and applauded through our school systems currently. In fact, many students get punished when they find it difficult to sit still enough to read, or the numbers on math worksheets seem to switch places, or they would much rather be outside in nature or moving their bodies, or they can't stop humming that chorus of the last song they heard. Our standardized system is not set up for many types of intelligences. It is extra important for us as parents, then, to show we value the areas our children have strengths in, even if they are not valued in school.

One thing I find especially interesting about this idea is that, as a society, we currently value reading, writing, and linguistic/mathematical intelligences, but things like interpersonal intelligence and creativity are gaining value in a variety of places. We are running into problems as a species that are taking every ounce of our creative problem-solving skills and teamwork to keep up with. Top-notch school admissions teams are telling the world that they care less about grades and more about other traits like creativity, problem solving, motivation, drive, dedication, teamwork, communication, and outside-the-box thinking.

It is presumptuous for us to think we know what information our children will need when they are adults. Teachers told past generations they needed to learn arithmetic because they would never have a calculator in their pocket. As I'm writing this, I have one in my pocket, one on my desk, and one in the bag beside me. That prediction did not come to fruition. We do not know what skills will lead to success in the future. If our parents had tried to predict that, they would be wrong on many counts. It is much more valuable for our kids to know things that can be generalized to many situations; things like assertiveness, resilience, optimism, self-esteem, trusting and healthy relationships, and how they learn best.

We need to problem-solve, embrace diversity, work together, and find solutions. With this in mind, creativity and curiosity are probably the two most important qualities we can foster. Ivy league schools are beginning to recognize this. Massively successful organizations are looking for this in their hiring process. Supporting our kids in their passions helps develop these important traits, even when their interests don't seem to align with our currently valued intelligence types, or the way they pursue their interest doesn't match our picture of it. We need to embrace diverse ways of doing and thinking. We'll do better as a society and a world if we do. Studies show that we solve problems better with a diverse group of people, for example, groups with a member with ADHD solve the problem significantly faster than the groups without.

Let's help our kids be uniquely themselves—trusting their voice, their direction, and understanding that learning happens everywhere if we can get out of the way and facilitate. Connections happen. One thing leads to another. Not everything will lead to a career, nor should it. Connections are not wasted. Learning how to play the piano when they are eight helps with brain development that factors in when they are 16. The eye-hand coordination they develop as a result of playing Fortnite when they are 12 doesn't go away when they turn 15. Skills translate, concepts connect, and those links matter. It is okay if they play the piano a little bit at eight years old and do not become a concert pianist for a career. Try not to put that sort of pressure on everything. Just because they didn't "make something" out of that interest does not mean they didn't benefit from it. We sometimes get this idea that we have to spend years on a topic to get benefits, but sometimes what we get can happen after just a taste.

When I was 13-18 years old, I was heavily invested in our community's ceramics department. I threw probably thousands of pounds of clay every year, loving to throw cups in particular. I made hundreds of cups on the wheel. I loved everything about it. I can close my eyes now and instantly have the feel of clay through my fingers, the rough wheel under my hands, the smell of Soldate 60 and the damp feel of wet clay on my pant legs from wiping my hands between projects. I love wheel throwing maybe more than anything else in the world. The process of making a cup is to wedge the clay, throw the form on the wheel, trim and attach a handle, do a bisque firing, glaze it, and do a final firing in the kiln. I respect thoughtful glazers. I love a beautiful glaze. I couldn't care less about glazing my own cups. My cups would stack up at the bisque ware stage. I would have a locker full of unglazed vessels. Sometimes I would give them away to other people in the studio to glaze for me. I just did not care once I wasn't throwing it. Some people would say I was giving up, and that I needed to do the whole thing from start to finish. But I got what I wanted to get out of that experience once I was done with the wet clay. And that was enough.

My sister is having fun this year with baking. She's working her way around the world with new and different bakes. She is deriving tremendous amounts of satisfaction from baking, but to her, baking and decorating are two different things. Much like the glaze on my ceramics, she is not interested in decorating cookies or frosting cakes. And that's okay. If she had a parent telling her that she was giving up, or forcing her into frosting 36 sugar cookies, she would quickly become resentful and probably not want to do any part of it for much longer. Not frosting the cookies and not glazing the cups does not take away from the benefits derived from baking and throwing.

If you find yourself consistently upset that your child isn't finishing their projects or "following through," it is time to stop and ask yourself what they are getting out of the parts they have done. It is a fine line between supporting someone's interest and pushing your own agenda. Remember, our children are allowed to have their own experiences of the world. If we can support that and get our expectations out of the way, we might even learn a few things.

Sometimes we get invested because it is an interest area of our own, or we had such a specific and special introduction to this topic that we want very badly to make sure our kids have an equally wonderful experience. This is a trap! For example, I love all things Harry Potter. I am the right age to have read them and enjoyed the books as they came out. I experienced the thrill of midnight readings and watching as the theme parks got built, and seeing a whole universe become created. My children are born into a world where this already exists. They've already seen Harry Potter Lego videos and they have been to Universal Studios. So, as much as I would like to, I cannot control their introduction into one of my favorite fictional worlds. I have to let that be okay, and beyond that, I have to be excited for them to experience it all on their own. This part of their life is not about my experience of it.

Some kids do get turned off if you try to make it more than it is. For those kids, there are ways for eager parents to support their kids on the down low. Think of it as creating an environment conducive to their interest, rather than leading them through a program relating to their interest. It's like the difference between going to the tide pools to explore, rather than leading them on a guided tour of the aquarium.

What books could you add to the bookshelf, or stack on the back of the toilet?

What sort of cool odds or ends could you bring in and leave on the counter?

Any new posters or printouts you could put on the wall?

Who could you invite over to dinner who might have some neat and related stories?

Try not to lurk and watch to see if your child picks up the offered bait. Let your challenge be in finding a variety of interesting things to strew; don't make success hinge on their reception. Some things are a slow burn. Some things aren't about the specific item, but about the fact that your attitude is a supportive one.

It is also important for us to remember that children don't learn across areas in equal amounts. I have one child who was incredibly physically precocious—this child was climbing and jumping and running and hitting balls with bats at a quality and quantity that astounded me. While he was busy developing these kinesthetic skills, it makes sense that other areas were not necessarily matching pace. His brain and body were busy! One of his best friends was reading and noticing numbers long before mine was caring about those things. It also made sense that his friend was not developing physical skills in the same way mine was! There is so much development in such a short time in children that sometimes it is hard to remember that they really aren't doing it all at the same time. Try to notice what your children *are* doing, rather than what they aren't.

When we are talking about fields of interest that are commonly divided into subjects in school, it's also important to remember that we don't learn across those subjects equally either, and systems that try to make us do that are fighting a losing, and sort of ridiculous, battle.

If each subject was a bar on a graph, we don't learn History to a 30, then stop and go to Math until we've reached 30, then pause and go focus on Science until that's caught up to a 30 too. Learning does not look like that!

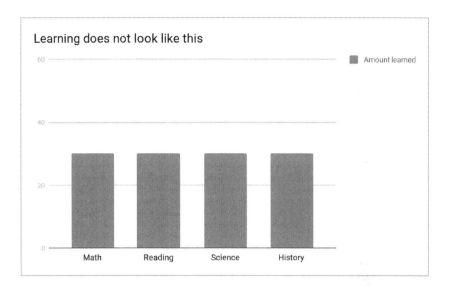

We could say it looks more like this, if you freeze time for a random kid:

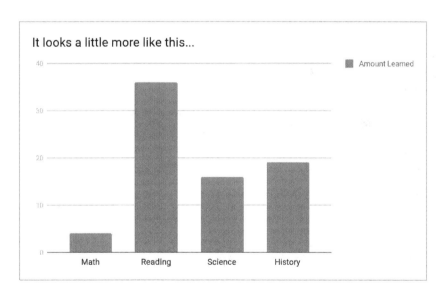

Even that isn't really an accurate picture, although maybe it's closer. We learn different things at different times, despite our public school system's attempts and desire to standardize education and subjects. It's how brains work. It's how learning works. And it's a good thing! Having a world full of people with different strengths, learning styles, capabilities, interests, and expertise is a really wonderful thing. For parents who mostly agree with that but think that everyone should at least start with a certain foundational base (let's say a 10 across the board on that chart, and then they are okay with fluctuations), I want to remind them that this idea of separating life into subjects is an incredibly arbitrary one.

The world is connected. Topics are connected. When I pick up a new knitting pattern, for example, I have to figure out my gauge swatch (math), I am looking at the yarn itself (Where was it made? Geography. How was it made? Science. How much money do I have to spend on yarn? Finance.). We learn better when we let those inter-subject connections happen, as they naturally do. I could go further with that knitting example. I could look up the pattern designer and find they live in another country, and then learn about that region, about different ways of shipping yarn to my location, about custom laws and international policies, about the economics and politics involved with exporting fiber, about the history of socks, cultural traditions, social justice and labor issues, etc. The list goes on and on. I am also learning non-school-subject related things, like how I deal with frustration, or how I like to learn new skills, or the feeling of mastery over a new technique. These are important things and will translate into other areas of my life.

When we divide all of the information the world has to offer into subjects, we cut ourselves off from seeing the learning that happens overall. We also forget that sometimes kids are learning in ways that are unobservable from the outside gaze. The good news is that those subject divisions are arbitrary and adult-made. When kids get up to a 30 in column A and are allowed to do that without shame or pressure, they are learning skills that translate to the other columns—if we need to see the world in those columns at all.

When we look for the areas our kids brains are focused on, rather than the places we feel they are deficient or behind in, we switch our thought process from a scared, negative, and potentially damaging one to a place where we can look at our kids with pride and wonder, and eliminate a few more barriers to positive relationships with our kids.

So, a bar graph isn't a great visual. It inherently creates a power dynamic, where we see some things as being more and others as being less. Maybe it's more like this:

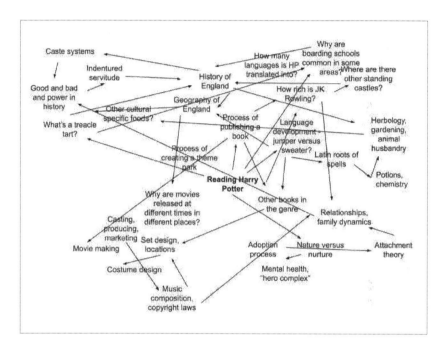

If I cared to reinforce subject delineations, I see a variety in this picture: geography, social studies, history, language, economics, political science, psychology, science, chemistry, etc. But even this is an incredibly incomplete visual.

Exercise 4

Create your own map of connections.

Start with your child's main interest point, such as Harry Potter, or Hatchimals, or Fortnite, or slime. Then add potential connections—either that you are seeing, or that you can imagine.

DABBLING CAN BE DELICIOUS

Even when we think that our children have narrow interests, when we look at all of the potential connections, we can see how depth can also lead to breadth.

Sometimes the interest will stay in the same general realm, such as Harry Potter in my example. Other times those connections will jump ship, continents, universes. The same principle applies.

Have you read *If You Give a Pig a Pancake?* It's a delightful children's book written by Laura Numeroff and is such a great metaphor for how to follow (or not) a kid's interest and the perspective you can have about it. So, in this book, the pig wants pancakes, and that leads to syrup, that leads to bath time, that leads to walks and writing letters and building tree houses and playing music—all sorts of activities. Each page is full of objects—flying, scattered, piled, energetic stacks of things. Some people might look at those illustrations and think, 'Eek! What a mess! What a terrible, scattered, haphazard way of living!' The moral of the story for them might be to be more orderly and contained, "Do one thing, clean it up, then do the next."

Some people might think that the book is a story of failure because they never did sit down and enjoy those delicious pancakes. I look at that and see a story of a wonderful friend and support person. Someone who sees their friend's interests changing and goes all out to support them. You have to change your definition of success.

If your definition of success is to eat five pancakes, then you will feel you have failed. But if your definition of success is to have an exciting day, you will have succeeded. So much depends on your perspective and being willing to change the barometer of success or failure. These two friends in this kid's book made connections. They learned things. They had adventures. They tasted new things. They worked with their hands. They practiced their linguistic skills. They spent time together. They played games. They improved their social skills. They experienced physical benefits. They did so many valuable things all day long because there was no person or schedule telling them it was time to stop and go back, to stop and clean up, to stop and switch gears. No person was imposing their own values or fears about order, cleanliness, control, or subject material on them.

Dabbling is okay. It is not wasted time. If that pancake-loving pig had decided to stop on page three and spend the next six months deeply immersed in letter-writing, that also would not have been wasted time.

Making a child stick out a class, team, or activity that they are now miserable in is another way we often (out of the goodness of our hearts) show our kids that we are not listening, paying attention, or caring about their interests.

It's especially hard to let a kid stop "midway" if we have spent money on it. We want to teach kids that sticking out an experience to the end is important. We think that it teaches discipline, stick-to-itiveness, and determination. It teaches our kids that hard work pays off. Now is a good time to point out, again, that children do not always learn what we think we are teaching.

I see parents pushing their kids to stay involved in things even when they are experiencing discomfort, distress, or unhappiness. But when we tell kids that it's more important to stay involved—even when their feelings, intuition, and experience is saying "Leave!"—we are essentially telling them that they should not trust themselves.

And that is a message that I see played out as a therapist every day. Distrusting your own experience, staying in something just because you have expended resources like money or time, even when you're miserable, sounds to me like the thought process that keeps many people in abusive relationships.

Determination and drive are great qualities, but your relationship with your kid is more important—and it is more valuable in this instance to figure out how to help them. The reason *why* they are miserable is a crucial factor. It is important to have a relationship with your child where they feel comfortable telling you those reasons and trust that you are going to pay attention and listen. You taking their preferences seriously means they are more likely to take you seriously when you talk about how things are sometimes difficult, and some difficult things are worth working through. Struggle is not always negative. Sometimes, when things are hard, we can use tools to get better. Sometimes the reward for sticking with a difficult situation or task is worth the strife along the way. This lesson is more effectively taught if they know you are not going to brush off their feelings about the difficulty just because you paid money upfront.

Pay attention to the patterns of your specific child. If you know your child has a habit of being really invested in something for about one week and then wants to topic-hop, it seems almost cruel to know this and require they stay in a program for longer than that. Classes and workshops are not the only way to experience an interest. This is another opportunity for creative thinking. Developmentally, most kids just are not equipped to make promises that involve the future. Don't put them in that position. It sets everyone up for distress later, and you're the adult; you could have prevented that.

Look for the pitfalls you know will come along. If your child is likely to stay interested in something for a few weeks and tells you they want to join a team for longer than that, it is time for a lot of conversation. It's time to talk about how joining a team impacts other people. It's time to talk about realistic time expectations. It's time to talk about the opportunity cost: what they will have to miss to make it to practice / shows / games / rehearsals. It's time to have those conversations, and also not expect them to be able to hold themselves to a promise or contract of completion. We start the conversations, but again, it isn't until we are into adulthood that we're developmentally able to look at things from others' perspectives. Help protect your kids from situations like this.

Teach them to trust their conscience, their voice, their intuition, their experience, their truth, their inner whatever you want to call it.

Let them know that if they want to start something, it's okay to stop. That's how we explore. That's how we expose ourselves to a variety of topics and connections. What I often see happening is children whose parents make them stick it out to the bitter end eventually stop *starting* things. There is too great a risk they will dislike it. And knowing their parents make them continue, they never start things. That is one of the saddest things I see on a regular basis.

Remember, just because they express an interest, it does not mean you have to rush out and sign them up for a class / team / workshop. The pig with the pancakes got to move from thing to thing because he wasn't stuck in a six-week breakfast-foods-making course. Maybe that could come later if that turned out to be an enduring interest. Being able to think creatively about other ways to support the pig's—and your kid's—interests is part of what this book is for.

Supporting that pig would be harder to do if you had two, three, four, or more pigs asking for pancakes, yes. It would be harder to do if your partner really opposed coming home to a messy house. It would be harder to do if you didn't have very much money to buy stamps, or supplies for building, or have space for a treehouse. There are barriers, yes. But logistics can be worked out. Your perspective about what defines success and how you can support your children; those are mental exercises you can do regardless of your privilege or resources.

I hope this section has helped solidify what you already know in your bones to be true: children's interests deserve to be protected and supported, and you, the adult, are the one who gets to figure out how. This is big stuff, even when it's in the guise of something lighthearted or frivolous. It impacts their well-being, their mental health, their self-esteem, their cognitive development, and their relationship with you.

The following sections are going to keep on along the same idea. What happens when things go wrong and passions are not protected? What happens when it goes right? What are some specific tools you can use to overcome your barriers to supporting your children? It is all here for you to explore and put into practice. Enjoy enjoying your children.

SECTION II

WHAT HAPPENS WHEN THINGS GO
WRONG

PLAY A GAME WITH ME

I want to talk to you about what happens when parents don't support their child's interests and illustrate how important it is. I have a lot of stories, given the nature of my work as a therapist. However, I cannot write about my clients, nor would I want to make light of their process.

Most of my book focuses on the good that can happen when you connect with your children and protect their passions. The reverse is also true—the evidence is all around us. When a parent does not honor, support, and protect their child's interests, the impact can be devastating.

Given the serious damage that can be done, I want to take a bit of a lighter approach and turn this into a game! I like games, and I love the storytelling that can happen through television and movies. This section is going to involve both!

The next few pages have brief vignettes of characters in movies and television looking back at their childhood. Try to guess who it is before reading the answers at the end. Here's a clue: characters 1-9 are fairytales/Disney and 10-12 are from other television shows.

Each character would have had better relationships and healthier self-esteem had their parents and support systems been more connected with them and protected their passions.

One

My dad had a lot of fears about my interests (marine biology and boating), so I wasn't allowed to have anything to do with them. I loved my dad and wanted him to be happy with me, so I deeply internalized that there was something wrong with me for being interested in the ocean!

I was lucky—I had another mentor who encouraged me to pursue my interests. Ultimately, I was able to prove to my dad how valuable my interests could be. But I think sadly of the years I felt disconnected from him, and I wish he had taken steps to deal with his fears earlier.

Two

My parents were so fearful of my special talents that they spent a lot of energy denying, dismissing, and ultimately squashing them out of me. It was a terrible, cold time. I was scared because my parents believed these talents were bad and would hurt others, so I isolated myself.

It impacted my relationships and my identity—the core of who I was. I wish my parents had realized they were acting out of fear and sending me the message that there was something wrong with me. Yes, I did accidentally hurt my sister once. But if my parents had supported me by finding resources and opportunities to learn safer ways to use my talents, I would have learned to love myself and could have had better relationships with the people around me—especially my sister.

Three

My dad was such a strong supporter of my quirks growing up.

He was a quirky, eccentric guy himself, and it was just the two of us living in a small, provincial town. I was so lucky to have him, especially since nobody else in my town was supportive. It would have been so powerful if more adults around me had the same outlook as my dad. Instead I grew up feeling really different; believing I was strange and alone. My whole town was judgemental. I felt ostracized and increasingly desperate. Ultimately, I made the rash decision to live with a frightening stranger in an unfamiliar place. I think about how the whole town could have changed for the better if more people supported their kids' quirky interests.

Four

My parents died in a car crash when I was young. It was very traumatic. I had issues with child protective services, our house caught fire—it was a scary, chaotic time. I was so lucky that my parents had supported my deep love for Elvis music and photography and that they had instilled that supportive instinct in my one remaining caregiver: my older sister. I credit being able to turn to the things I loved in those terrible times with my resilience and ability to continue forming healthy relationships. I think it's so important for parents to support their kids' interests and help build their self-esteem, even when those interests seem a bit unusual or even bizarre.

Five

My step-mother was undeniably abusive to me growing up. As an adult, I can better understand how her deep-seated fears led to her terrible treatment of me, although it has taken me years to get to that point. If she had dealt with her clearly terrible childhood and resulting misguided ideas about parenting, cleanliness, and chores, she might have been better able to parent me from a place of understanding and compassion. Instead, she lived in fear, which translated into aggression and abuse in the form of housework and social isolation. In turn, I became passive and felt unable to escape, existing in a world of wishful thinking.

Six

I had such weird interests growing up! No one in my family knew what to do with me. It would have been funny if it weren't so tragic. I felt so alone, yet so driven by my passions that I did elaborate things to hide them. I had secret stashes and met up with strangers. I look back and shudder, thinking about some of the dangerous situations I got myself into. If my dad had understood and supported me, we could have built my collection together. He could have used his considerable resources to connect me with knowledgeable people, showing me that I could trust him to be supportive. It could have brought us closer together. Instead, it drove a wedge between us and put me in some sketchy situations. I will definitely need to work through this as an adult so that I don't do the same to my kids.

Seven

I was deeply passionate about music, especially playing the guitar. Not only did my family not support my interest, they actively worked against it, citing family tradition and past negative experiences. I felt torn apart, internalizing that this thing I loved was bad and therefore I must be bad. It led me to feel like I couldn't trust my otherwise wonderful, close, and loving family. I resorted to secrecy and vandalism, seeking connection in groups of other people. Some of them were dangerous and scary and I put myself in harm's way.

Eight

I had a very adventurous spirit, and always wanted to explore and see what was around the corner! I was a physical kid, but due to a loss in my dad's past, he was fearful and discouraged me from taking risks. Because of that, I wasn't shown how to navigate risky situations and I built up a lot of resentment toward my dad. When given the chance, I took what turned out to be a huge risk and endangered several people that I loved. I wish my dad had supported my interests and provided a safety net while I explored, so that I could have taken developmentally appropriate risks with his help.

Nine

My mother prioritized other things over our relationship. I know she had troubles and struggled with her mental health, but, as a kid, I felt like I couldn't do anything because of how it might reflect on her. Although she brought me things to occupy my time, she did not believe my real interests were valuable or important, so I was restricted. I wanted her to love me so I tried to be happy where I was, but my boredom led me to jumping too quickly into a serious relationship in order to escape. It launched me down a path that was difficult to navigate since I had never really learned to trust myself, or how to have a healthy intimate partnership.

Ten

I was an expert in my field, even as a teenager. My parents were afraid of my passion and had a lot of preconceived biases against the people involved. It was a high stakes interest, and I had to be very physical, training for hours a day. Even when it took up more and more of my time, my parents wouldn't talk about it. Even when things went wrong and I had to move, my parents wouldn't talk about it. It got to the point where my parents—especially my mom —were in such denial that I could really only share my inner life with a few close friends. It would have been amazing if they had been supportive: helping me train; setting up a studio for me; and paying for martial arts lessons. Instead, I hid my immense strength and abilities—my true self—from them. I had a series of questionable relationships and suffered from low self-esteem for years. It took a long time for me to realize that I was capable of being a leader.

Eleven

As an adult, my low self-esteem translated into extreme passivity. I had a hard time asking for what I wanted and going after my goals. I would have liked to be an artist and to live somewhere beautiful in a house with a verandah. I did not know how to listen to my inner voice, and that meant I stayed in a serious relationship for years, even when I knew we weren't right together. I let things happen to me, rather than making things happen—until I discovered what it felt like to be supported in my interests. I pursued higher education, took classes in my interests, and, with every new accomplishment, became more and more assertive.

Twelve

The people around me constantly made fun of me for my life's passion; paleontology. I studied it, taught it, and made a career out of it. I was so well-respected that I was invited to speak at international conferences, and yet my friends and family still dismissed my interest as childish or inconsequential. It affected my self-esteem, and I rushed into relationships because I was desperate for approval. It's evident that some of my developmental growth was negatively impacted and, as a result, I continued to live out a pattern of poor decisions for years.

"We were both concerned about how much time our boys spent playing video games and watching YouTube videos, so I started to seek out wise advice from seasoned parents who had close relationships with their kids. It wasn't always easy, but when it got hard, we reminded ourselves that we wanted to keep our relationship with our kids (instead of fear) at the forefront of all our interactions. We became their allies rather than their enemies, and that has made all the difference."

— JULIE

$\sim$

OVER AND OVER AGAIN, we see heartbreaking evidence that dismissing or undervaluing children's passions is the norm in popular culture. Art imitates life, as they say, and it can be heartbreaking to watch. Moana's father's resistance is a plot point to illustrate the depth of her longing, but I think an entire movie could be made about their relationship. Ross Gellar is a slapstick comedic character that is problematic in a lot of ways, but when I stop to think about what it would be like to live in a group of friends who constantly mock me for my interests? I ache for that fictional character.

Hurt people hurt others. Whether it's with scoffing language, not taking the time to show them that we value their interests, or not making the effort to show them that we understand the details— when we dismiss people's passions, we are showing the people around us that we do not value them. Television shows and movies are full of examples of the negative things that can happen as a result.

It wouldn't make for a great movie, but if Moana's father had seen her interest at a young age and chosen to show her how to sail and how to navigate by reading the stars and the currents, how quickly could she have solved her island's problems? If Ariel's father had taken two minutes to get to know why she was so fascinated by human objects, if he had listened to her sing about her collection, if he had seen the amazing potential in her curating prowess, she might not have felt desperate enough to turn to the sea witch, putting everyone in danger. She could have had a close and connected relationship with her father and turned to him for help instead.

$\sim$

THE ANSWERS!

    One: Moana

    Two: Elsa (Frozen)

    Three: Belle (Beauty and the Beast)

    Four: Lilo (Lilo & Stitch)

    Five: Cinderella

    Six: Ariel (The Little Mermaid)

    Seven: Miguel (Coco)

    Eight: Nemo (Finding Nemo)

    Nine: Rapunzel (Tangled)

    Ten: Buffy Summers (Buffy the Vampire Slayer)

    Eleven: Pam Beasley (The Office)

    Twelve: Ross Gellar (Friends)

SECTION III

WHAT HAPPENS WHEN THINGS GO RIGHT

EMBRACE THE LITTLE MOMENTS

Our culture subscribes to a particular image of teenagers: they are sullen, resistant, isolated, and angry. They pierce things and hide in their rooms, turning into strangers to their parents. It's usually at this point that parents send their kids to me to "fix them" or "turn them back into how they used to be." Parents are sometimes baffled by this change. Others expect it, so it feels almost normal; just a phase to survive.

This negative picture is completely unnecessary. Yes, certain times of our lives are dedicated to individualizing, separating from our family of origin and striking out on our own. And other times we may value our social support more than our familial support, but the idea that teens have to turn into monsters is absolutely make-believe. Separation can happen without conflict. Growing up can happen without rifts in the family. I know this because I have spent thousands of hours with families where this was the case. I have also read, watched, and studied the differences between these families and those where there is rampant strife through the teen years.

When things go right in a big way, it is the result of many small moments being done right. "Right" looks different depending on the situation, but it always involves respect, connection, communication, appreciation, and enjoyment.

How do we find all of the little moments that build toward the big ones? Through our children's play and interests. When we protect their passions, the benefits are vast. They are beautiful, radical, and fly in the face of conventional *kids-will-turn-into-terrible-teens* lore.

Generosity

When we provide ample support and resources to our kids, we are setting the stage for future generosity. It is not a perfect one to one exchange; this is a fruit that parents expect will ripen long before it actually does. When you generously give your children whatever they need to fulfill their passions—whether it is space, time, rides, equipment, laundry, headphones, glue, or lots of little toys—it influences how they interact with others and has a ripple effect.

Little kids with an abundance of Play-Doh invite their friends to play with them. It is when they only have a small amount, or if they are worried that their Play-Doh might get taken away, that they tighten their grasp and are afraid to give. Even parents without a lot of financial or material resources can provide abundance in other ways. When we feel restricted, we restrict as well. When we experience expansiveness and generosity, we feel more like giving. It is a wonderful side benefit of supporting your child's interests through providing materials, tools, space, and time.

Creativity

I had a ceramics teacher who told us to make at least 100 of any item that we were learning to make. She said that if we made fewer than that, we would become miserly, wanting too badly for them to be "successful" and be too tentative to experiment. Having more than enough for trial and error was vital for making mistakes without fear.

Now, imagine your child believes you don't really approve of their interest, yet knows they need to rely on you for supplies. They probably won't want to take many risks with it, will they? Creativity is an incredibly vital trait for individuals, both from a personal and societal perspective. We need creativity for everything but unfortunately, this is a characteristic that research shows we are losing across the board. We are exhibiting less creativity than we did a decade ago, and less than the decade before that, but our need for creativity has not diminished. Supporting your children might mean providing them with "more than enough" materials, time, and supplies because they need enough to ruin, destroy, experiment, explore, try out, practice, fool around with, make mistakes, and use in a variety of ways.

Learn How to Fail

Learning how to fail is part of the creative process and another valuable experience. What do we gain when we learn how to fail? We gain optimism and resiliency. We try new things, then we try them again. We learn from experience. We learn how to ask for help. We find tools, resources, and allies. Through all of that, we learn about ourselves and how and when we work best. We learn that struggle is not the end of us. We build strength. We practice doing hard things. We practice positive self-talk. We learn that often the process is as important as the end result. We learn new skills, glean new facts, discover innovative ways of doing things, and gain new insights about ourselves and the world around us.

Attract Mentors

People responsible for hiring employees have told me many times that "skills can be taught, but attitude cannot." Think about the people you are attracted to helping and supporting. They usually share some of these traits: they are motivated, engaged, open-minded, and curious to learn more. They take the initiative, and work hard.

When we support our kids interests, we are helping them develop these qualities, which may open up more opportunities for mentorship as they get older. More opportunities for mentors leads to more learning, more success, and more opportunities.

Insisting that our children participate in activities they are not interested in or disparaging their current passions encourages apathy and passivity, which are among the least attractive traits for potential mentors and employers. Through our actions, they learn that caring and trying their best is not worth it. We can help find mentors by helping our children *live out loud* through their interests. We help them do that by making sure they know that what they're doing is valuable and worth sharing.

Experience Exponential Growth of Opportunities

I have heard many stories from parents who are helping their children know and show their worth in this way. Many have found their way into the workforce through their area of interest because someone else took notice. For example, my sister, Rose was passionate about karate. Our parents found a supportive studio and took her to extra practices and demo team performances, spending money and years of their time supporting her interest. The woman who ran the studio noticed Rose's initiative and eventually hired her. Fast forward to the present and she is teaching at a college level, thanks, in large part, to her early teaching experience as a karate instructor.

Then there is my lifelong friend Kirby, who enjoyed playing Pokémon at his local game shop, often staying late to help put away the tables and chairs. When he saw a need, he stepped up and volunteered to organize the Pokémon games for a few months. The next time they were hiring, they offered him a job, making him the youngest employee at the game store. He went on to work for a major video game company. He credits his success to his passion for games and the fact that he only seeks out work environments that he enjoys.

My own experience with intensely following my passions has led to educational and research opportunities, employment, travel, and recreational prospects, new relationships, and much more.

Learn How to Learn

Being encouraged to pursue their interests provides a wealth of opportunities for kids. It can open doors and lead them down exciting and fruitful paths, but we don't know, as parents, exactly what those paths will hold. The specific knowledge they gain from their interests might not transfer to their career later in life, but there are skills and traits that will. Parental support leads to a finely-honed sense of *how* they learn.

One of the things that this group of people have in common is time—parents who let them spend vast amounts of time following their interests. The way we segment the school day in most public schools—with bells signalling the end to a subject every 45 minutes or so—is not conducive to diving deeply into any area of interest. Parents who give their children many hours of self-directed time see something else happen: their kids learn how they like to learn. They know themselves better because they are doing so much learning through experimenting and exploration, rather than having their educational path fed to them in bite-sized chunks. Because what's being taught isn't often connected to their interests, they are less engaged, which means less retention of the material. When a kid is increasingly in charge of their time, they can figure out so much about how they best receive and retain information. They know if they prefer to take in written information or video. They know they prefer to do new things in the morning and watch reruns in the evening when they've reached a saturation point. They know they need to be hands-on, or that they want to read all of the instructions before they start.

Many kids who go through the traditional public school environment have not had much time to figure out how they learn best because they were expected to learn using whatever process their teachers required. As a college professor, I often see this backfire. I've had students in my classes who are incapable of time management, or of taking the initiative to conduct their research, or to study. This means I have to backtrack and provide life management tools when we could be delving into my class content instead. Learning how we learn is a benefit that permeates every aspect of our lives, and parents who support their kids' interests are giving them a clear head start. It does not matter if they learn them through playing Minecraft, Pokémon, Shopkins, or Lego. They are valuable, transferable skills.

Develop Expertise

Have you ever talked to someone who is an expert in their field? Or someone who is genuinely passionate about a topic? They can ramble on for hours. Or maybe they get really loud and speak really fast. Details that seem insignificant to the rest of us make them light up, wave their hands around, and are clearly of monumental importance to them. I always find it uplifting to know there are people with deep knowledge and passion, even if I am not very fond of that specific topic.

When we help protect children's passions, we are also helping them learn mountains of fascinating information specific to their areas of interest! This can be the foundation of a career, new and lasting friendships, and a sense of expertise, all of which are valuable things. While we can rest assured that the skills our kids are learning are transferable to other situations, we may also discover that there are benefits to learning about the topic ourselves. Learning is fun. Having knowledge can be great. Supporting your kid as they dive into topics that they're particularly interested in can be so satisfying—for both of you.

Better Relationships with Parents

One of the common traits I see in healthy parent-child relationships is that the parent expends specific, conscious energy to build a healthy, connected relationship with their child, rather than a walled-off one. When they have the choice between two actions or attitudes, they take the route that puts their relationship first. There are many important reasons to put your relationship with your child above all other things. A big one is to foster their trust in you so that they know they can look to you to help guide them through challenging moments in their life. Another of the incredible benefits of supporting a kid in their passions is that it is a concrete way to put more energy toward building that bridge between you. This pays off handsomely as the stakes get higher. Every time you ask them lovingly about something they love, they see that it is safe to trust you with this information. Some day, they might need to trust you (they will need to trust you) with moments or information that makes them feel incredibly vulnerable. When that time comes, it behooves you both to have built a strong relationship—one based on lots of smaller, trusting moments.

When someone speaks disparagingly about your interest or otherwise demonstrates that they think it is meaningless or damaging, a part of you becomes closed off to them. If they don't listen or value your feelings, you won't trust them as much as you would like to. The typical refrain, "My parents just don't understand," doesn't come up in families where parents actively support their children's interests and put their relationships first. In these families, kids excitedly seek out their parents to show them new things. They also turn to their parents for comfort and refuge when things go wrong, and they ask their opinions and value their advice. Everyone benefits.

Better Mental Health

A parent's level of engagement has been shown through many studies, from many fields of research, to be an essential factor in a child's mental health and resiliency. On every level, supporting your child's interest benefits them. When you show that you trust them, you are demonstrating that they are trustworthy and modeling for them how to trust themselves. A sense of self-trust is critical for self-esteem, assertiveness, and trusting their judgement in challenging situations.

Providing opportunities to learn more in an area of interest can also lead to a sense of belonging—both physically and metaphorically. I have heard so many stories of people who say they found "home" or "another family" in their ceramics studio, dance group, or swim team. Having a sense of belonging in a place that supports you in your pursuit of bettering your skills is a powerful thing. Being able to walk through a studio and understand how the equipment is used, or to walk through a barn and know the behavior of each horse, leads to a strong sense of mastery. Arriving at the location each day and knowing what needs to happen to get it all going—that sense of belonging leads to greater self-esteem, self-worth, and self-efficacy.

When we feel connected to a place and other people, especially when they are working toward a similar goal, we feel connected to something bigger than ourselves. That is another interesting and critical aspect of healthy development; one that's valuable for working through depression, anxiety, and other mental illnesses or disorders. Feeling like our contribution matters helps us in many ways. If your child struggles with depression, anxiety, or other mental health issues, often that impacts their ability or desire to get up and out. Helping them pursue the things they are interested in can help with motivation, even when their depressed or anxious state is saying not to try. The activities, the people involved, the sense of mastery, all of that can be helpful when living with anxiety or depression.

Decreased Substance Abuse

One of the interesting things we see is that children who are actively engaged in recreational activities try fewer drugs or substances. There is less need to find a means of escape when you're enjoying your days. When your social circle revolves more around interests than school, it naturally includes a variety of ages, experience, and wisdom. Teenagers often start drinking or doing drugs due to a lack of perspective: if things feel terrible now, and their only support circle feels the same way, then escapism becomes very appealing. If your teenager has a support circle around them who are older, younger, and all invested in the same activity, then they can see for themselves that there is life beyond their age cohort. They get perspective. They see a bigger picture. They see that other people have made it through difficult moments.

Better Learning Environment

Have you ever tried to learn when you were frustrated, resentful, bitter, or feeling forced? Not only are you much less likely to learn the material, you are more likely to associate that information with a feeling of coercion. It feels like a big lead weight on your shoulders. Curiosity, exploration, excitement, and joy are shut down. When we require kids to learn arbitrary things that are not of interest in their lives, we damage their desire to learn.

Early reading intervention, for example, frequently has the side effect of children declaring that they hate to read. These are the same children who love storytelling in other forms, and if left to their own wondrous discovery, would have probably developed a love of reading. In the 4th grade, we had to choose an animal to study, and I was so excited to study something from the ocean. I wanted to be a marine biologist and could not wait for this assignment. When the time came, they gave me the desert rat. The. Desert. Rat. As far from the kelp forest and sea lions as it was possible to be. I remember the sinking, cement feeling in my stomach as I looked at that terrible little rodent. What a wasted opportunity. What worlds they could have opened up for me had they followed my passion at the time; it would have been so easy to go from factual information about my favorite pinniped to learning more about science, geography, and history.

We learn better when we care. We learn better when we have choices. We learn better when we have room to explore what sparks our curiosity. We learn better when the people around us create an environment that supports those interests. When we can approach topics with time, space, freedom, and creativity, we are more able to integrate information, to make important connections, and to do it free of stress and anxiety.

SECTION IV

BARRIERS

BARRIERS

There can be many barriers to supporting your children's interests, and some of them can feel insurmountable. Maybe you just do not have the disposable income to buy the collectible toys they want every day! And what do you do when the nearest studio/rink/arena/location to do the activity is three hours away? How do you get them there every day for practice? And, even if you could do it, what if there are siblings who don't want to go along for that three-hour car ride?

Exercise 5

Take a minute to brainstorm all of the difficulties you see in supporting your children's interests. Be sure to write as many down as you can think of and get it out of your system. Let's look at what we are dealing with here.

You might have a list of 20 possible difficulties or barriers, to supporting them. Or, you might have one or two seemingly mountainous obstacles.

In my experience, these barriers fall into two big categories: logistical and emotional.

Let's look at my list and see how it compares to yours:

Logistical
Lack of time
Lack of money
Limited space
Limited resources
Other kids have needs
No one else does that around here
It's messy

Emotional
Their interest goes against my values
I don't see the value in what they're doing
I'm worried it will lead to their ruin
They won't be successful
I don't like it/it's boring
It's risky/dangerous
Opportunity cost: they're missing out on other important things
Judgement from others
They've only had one interest for years
They don't WANT us involved
I need "me" time

I've separated them into two categories—emotional and logistical—but, in actuality, this is what that list really looks like:

Emotional
Their interest goes against my values
I don't see the value in what they're doing

I'm worried it will lead to their ruin

They won't be successful

I don't like it/it's boring

It's risky/dangerous

Opportunity cost: they're missing out on other important things

Judgement from others

They've only had one interest for years

They don't WANT us involved

I need "me" time

Lack of time

Lack of money

Limited space

Limited resources

Other kids have needs

No one else does that around here

It's messy

See what I did there?

Even the barriers that appear mostly logistical are really emotional barriers when you go deep enough. When a person is wholly on board with supporting their kids' interests and that desire is genuine and strong, the logistical aspects feel less like barriers and more like challenges—they are opportunities for creative thinking and brainstorming. It's when we have some resistance to the interest itself that those "logistical" barriers loom large. When that happens, we succumb to the difficulty, turn off our creative thinking, stop looking for solutions, and throw our hands in the air, saying, "It's just too hard to make that happen!" But when we deal with the emotional piece first, it's amazing how creative and solution-oriented we can be.

For example, although your income level or the square footage of your apartment might feel like an obvious logistical barrier, look a bit deeper. How you choose to allocate money, space, time, and other resources are, in the bigger picture, statements of your values, and values are an emotional piece of the puzzle. The point of this book is not to shame you for where you choose to spend your resources, but to ask you to think carefully about those choices. To treat them as fascinating pieces of information about your perspective and inherent biases as they relate to supporting your kids. It's an exploration. We are going to strive to have all of the best qualities of an explorer as we do this work: curious, resilient, persistent, open-minded, questioning, connecting, documenting, archiving.

What happens if a barrier truly is such that you can't creatively think your way around it? Even if you have done the work and know with certainty that it is not due to your own inner resistance? Although those times are fewer than most people think, they can happen. The outcome changes dramatically based on your history with your child.

If you come to that insurmountable barrier with years of "good credit" with your child—years of showing them through many small actions that you support them, value them, and trust them—then they are much more forgiving of the times when something can't happen. Taking each little opportunity to connect with and support them is a way to bank credit—to build trust. If they trust you will do your best to help them make their interests happen, then on the odd occasion when something really is too hard, too dangerous, too whatever, they know it's reality. They know you are not arbitrarily withholding your support. And they are more likely to agree to creative solutions or adaptations, or to help come up with solutions themselves. But it does take years of proof to build that trust. If instead, you have a history of making rules, limiting choices, and enforcing strict policies that feel unfair or arbitrary to your child, then they won't trust that this time is different. Build good credit, not resentment.

"My confidence as a parent was shaken when my kids' interests were so outside of my comfort zone that I was faced with my own judgements and preconceived notions about things. When my son was just 7, he was interested in weightlifting. I was scared that he'd be injured and the vast majority of resources I found supported my fear-based approach to his interest. By digging deeper and looking for outside-the-box perspectives, I found I was able to explore my own fears and the ways that they manifest in my parenting. Some of it had to do with letting go of what others might think of me as a mother who allows a young child to weight lift. Some of it was confronting my fears about what I thought could happen to my son's body image. It was ALL my own stuff to work through. Without the voices and support of other parents who encouraged me to create space for my son's interest and to explore alongside him, I wouldn't have had the opportunity for personal growth that still guides my parenting now that he's 10."

— CLARISSA

BARRIER 1: MONEY

Where we decide to spend our money is a concrete representation of our values. Some people spend very little on entertainment through most of their lives but splurge on travel experiences. Others would never dream of taking a solo vacation but go on frequent family trips. Some will regularly spend money on haircuts or hair dye because self-expression, or feeling polished and taken care of, is important to them. Others put that value lower on their list and might instead choose to spend that money on something that satisfies their desire to host events, bring people together, or have new experiences. Even if people spend money on the same thing or experience, the meaning they make of it reflects their values. I might spend money each week on fancy coffee drinks because it's important to me to have social time with my friends. Someone else might spend the same amount of money on the same thing but, for them, it is about taking time to refresh themselves. One is not inherently better or more virtuous than the other, yet often we have been raised to believe that the values we grew up with are the best, while others are subpar.

Individuals come into any given situation with their own set of values, as do families. Most often, it is the adults of the family determining what the family value system will be. That works until it doesn't; which happens if the adults are actively ignoring the values of the other people in the family, misinterpreting them as flaws, or even disparaging them.

Exercise 6a

Below is a long list of values. Write down/cross off all but the top 20 values you think are the most important for people (in general) to have.

Once you have your top 20, cross off all but the top 10.

Cross off 5 more, leaving your top 5.

Extra credit exercise: do this through the eyes of each member of your family. What do you think *their* top values are?

Involve them, if they're game, and ask them to do this exercise. Compare what they chose as their top values with what you chose on their behalf.

Abundance
Acceptance
Accessibility
Accomplishment
Accuracy
Achievement
Acknowledgement
Activeness
Adaptability
Adoration
Adroitness
Adventure
Affection
Affluence
Aggressiveness
Agility
Alertness

Altruism
Ambition
Amusement
Anticipation
Appreciation
Approachability
Articulacy
Assertiveness
Assurance
Attentiveness
Attractiveness
Audacity
Availability
Awareness
Awe
Balance
Beauty
Being the best
Belonging
Benevolence
Bliss
Boldness
Bravery
Brilliance
Buoyancy
Challenge
Charity
Charm
Chastity
Cheerfulness
Clarity
Cleanliness
Clear-mindedness
Cleverness
Closeness

Comfort
Commitment
Compassion
Completion
Composure
Concentration
Confidence
Conformity
Congruency
Connection
Consciousness
Consistency
Contentment
Continuity
Contribution
Control
Conviction
Conviviality
Coolness
Cooperation
Cordiality
Correctness
Courage
Courtesy
Craftiness
Creativity
Credibility
Cunning
Curiosity
Daring
Decisiveness
Decorum
Calmness
Camaraderie
Candor

Capability
Care
Carefulness
Celebrity
Certainty
Deference
Delight
Dependability
Depth
Desire
Determination
Devotion
Devoutness
Dexterity
Dignity
Diligence
Direction
Directness
Discipline
Discovery
Discretion
Diversity
Dominance
Dreaming
Drive
Duty
Dynamism
Eagerness
Economy
Ecstasy
Education
Effectiveness
Efficiency
Elation
Elegance

Empathy
Encouragement
Endurance
Energy
Enjoyment
Entertainment
Enthusiasm
Excellence
Excitement
Exhilaration
Expectancy
Expediency
Experience
Expertise
Exploration
Expressiveness
Extravagance
Extroversion
Exuberance
Fairness
Faith
Fame
Family
Fascination
Fashion
Fearlessness
Ferocity
Fidelity
Fierceness
Financial independence
Firmness
Fitness
Flexibility
Flow
Fluency

Focus
Fortitude
Frankness
Freedom
Friendliness
Frugality
Fun
Gallantry
Generosity
Gentility
Giving
Grace
Gratitude
Gregariousness
Growth
Guidance
Happiness
Harmony
Health
Heart
Helpfulness
Heroism
Holiness
Honesty
Honor
Hopefulness
Hospitality
Humility
Humor
Hygiene
Imagination
Impact
Impartiality
Independence
Industry

Ingenuity
Inquisitiveness
Insightfulness
Inspiration
Integrity
Intelligence
Intensity
Intimacy
Intrepidness
Introversion
Intuition
Intuitiveness
Inventiveness
Investing
Joy
Judiciousness
Justice
Keenness
Kindness
Knowledge
Leadership
Learning
Liberation
Liberty
Liveliness
Logic
Longevity
Looking good
Love
Loyalty
Majesty
Making a difference
Mastery
Maturity
Meekness

Mellowness
Meticulousness
Mindfulness
Modesty
Motivation
Mysteriousness
Nature
Neatness
Nerve
Obedience
Open-mindedness
Openness
Optimism
Order
Organization
Originality
Outlandishness
Outrageousness
Passion
Peace
Perceptiveness
Perfection
Perkiness
Perseverance
Persistence
Persuasiveness
Philanthropy
Piety
Playfulness
Pleasantness
Pleasure
Poise
Polish
Popularity
Potency

Power
Practicality
Pragmatism
Precision
Preparedness
Presence
Privacy
Proactivity
Professionalism
Prosperity
Prudence
Punctuality
Purity
Realism
Reasonableness
Recognition
Recreation
Refinement
Reflection
Relaxation
Reliability
Religiousness
Resilience
Resolution
Resolve
Resourcefulness
Respect
Rest
Restraint
Reverence
Richness
Rigor
Ritual
Sacredness
Sacrifice

Sagacity
Saintliness
Sanguinity
Satisfaction
Security
Self-control
Selflessness
Self-reliance
Sensitivity
Sensuality
Serenity
Service
Sexuality
Sharing
Shrewdness
Significance
Silence
Silliness
Simplicity
Sincerity
Skillfulness
Solidarity
Solitude
Soundness
Speed
Spirit
Spirituality
Spontaneity
Spunk
Stability
Stealth
Stillness
Strength
Structure
Success

Support

Supremacy

Surprise

Sympathy

Synergy

Teamwork

Temperance

Thankfulness

Thoroughness

Thoughtfulness

Thrift

Tidiness

Timeliness

Traditionalism

Tranquility

Transcendence

Trust

Trustworthiness

Truth

Understanding

Unflappability

Uniqueness

Unity

Usefulness

Utility

Valor

Variety

Victory

Vigor

Virtue

Vision

Vitality

Vivacity

Warmth

Watchfulness

Wealth
Willfulness
Willingness
Winning
Wisdom
Wittiness
Wonder
Youthfulness
Zeal

What are your top 5 values?

What do you predict your partner's top 5 values are?

What did they choose?

What do you predict your children's top 5 values are? (Do for each of your children.)

What did they choose?

What values do you have in common?

Which ones are different?

Are there any that feel completely at odds with each other?

ONE THING I think is important to recognize is that while this is a very long list, it is still incomplete. There are hundreds of positive qualities you could choose from. You physically crossed off several hundred qualities and characteristics that did not make your top cut. That does not mean those several hundred other values are bad. It means that in your life, through your experiences, you **have** prioritized some over others.

People who are not you have prioritized a different set of values. That doesn't make those individuals bad people. It doesn't make them the opposite of your top values. Meaning, if you chose hard-working and your child didn't, it doesn't make them the opposite (lazy). They simply value other things more. It can be tempting to view people through our lens of values, but that hurts our relationships more than it helps. Instead, look at what they value and try to see how that is reflected in their choices.

Remember that your children are living by a set of values—some you might share, some might be lower on your list, and some might surprise you! This realization alone can help you shift your internal language about their choices. It will also help you clarify why you make the choices you do and highlight areas where your kids might not understand them.

When I was about 13, I was suddenly surrounded by friends in a way I hadn't been before. I was a member of a few different groups and teams, and as an incredibly social and extroverted person, I was in heaven. When I think about that time, I have wonderful memories. When my mother talks about that time, she mentions the struggles she and I had in places that used to be easy. She talks about how our conflicts increased, almost exclusively in one area: money. It would be easy to chalk that up to hormones, to becoming a teen, and this idea we seem to have that teenagers turn into cranky, unhelpful people almost overnight. My mom, however, paid attention to patterns and realized that over and over again, we were fighting because I wanted to buy gifts for my friends every time we went out. I would walk through any grocery store, gift shop, or shopping center, be reminded of my friends, and want to buy them something. My mother, not being able to afford daily gifts for my many teammates, was finding that she had to say no to me a lot more often than she had before. I would get angry, and we would fight. Hence, the increase in conflict.

If you look at this from a values perspective, it is much easier to see that I, as an exuberant and social teenager, was valuing my friendships and those connections and saw gift-giving as a sign of love and camaraderie. Those are values most parents would be happy to support generously. You might have to be creative about how, but you would probably want to approach it differently than saying, "No! Stop asking for money!" You might talk about other ways to show your friends you adore them. You might spend more time talking about your kid's friends. You might figure out how to give your child an allowance to spend on whatever they want—like random gifts for random people—so that they can make those choices based on their values and you can still feed your family. You might remind them that homemade gifts are thoughtful, or make lists of their birthdays and save gifts for that date, or help them create a wish list, or a myriad of other things. This path helps your child feel supported in their values and shows your willingness to meet them where they are, without draining your bank account at the same time.

I was lucky; my mom did do most of those things. But often I hear stories from parents that go more like, "My child has no understanding of life; I tell them no, and they keep asking. They just want, want, want, want, want. I am worried they are greedy and materialistic. They have so much stuff already. They have no appreciation for the value of things, how hard we work to earn money, or where the money needs to go. They don't care about our family. They are selfish. They are inconsiderate. They won't be able to manage money when they are older."

The stories I hear from their kids go more like, "My parents don't understand me. They don't listen to what I think is important. They don't know the names of my friends. I know I can't have all the money in the world, but they don't understand that I'd rather get my friends something than get a stupid new shirt, go out to eat with my family, or whatever. Everyone else is generous; I'm the one with the stingy parents. It's important to me, and they don't understand."

~

"Cheerleading Jayn's interests has been one of the foundations of our parenting success. Her interests have included solo activities like drawing, as well as games and play that have involved friends and her father and I. Each of these have been a window into her thinking. Her fascination with dolls of all kinds - including collecting - led me into the world of art dolls and textile art, creating a new business and arts practice that has endured even as Jayn's interests in dolls matured.

Now her interests in various games and media - particularly soundtracks - have taken her into professional aspirations. She is entering college to study Game Design and plans to ride to classes with Dad every day when he goes to work at the same school."

— ROBYN

WE SHIFT our values throughout our life. The first time I did a similar values exercise, I was in Girl Scouts at the ripe old age of seven. We stashed that piece of paper in a folder, and I found it about a decade later. I did the exercise again and laughed at both how much had changed, and how much had stayed the same. I put the date on that paper, and again, put it away in a folder...to find again another decade later. I now do this exercise more frequently because I do it each semester with my students, and in between with clients. My values have changed, as do all of ours, as our life shifts and our roles change. Your children and teenagers should not have values identical to yours. They really shouldn't, for their developmental health. If they did, I would wonder if they were acting too adult, too soon, and carrying too much responsibility. This is known as parentification and is generally seen as an unhealthy coping tool in the mental health profession.

Values align with our developmental life stages. It makes perfect sense for a teenager's values to reflect that they are stretching beyond their family of origin. They are supposed to be individuating; they are supposed to be exploring new ways of thinking; they are supposed to be finding a new support system with their friends. This doesn't make them bad people. It simply means they are valuing things differently than you.

It is important for us and our relationships to be able to find value in the things that the people we love value. Diversity is important for creativity, problem-solving, conflict management, richness, storytelling, and overall wellbeing. Within a family structure, diversity is as important as it is in the rest of the world. When babies start out as such a part of us, it's hard to let them be their own human beings as they get older. Yet, your life will be richer for it. Their life will be healthier for it. Look at their value system and rejoice in it.

Exercise 6b

What about this exercise feels surprising?

How do your children's values illustrate their strengths?

How do your children's choices of play and activities demonstrate their values?

Were there any values that were easy to eliminate?

What about for your partner or kids?

Were there any values that you "want to want" but that, truthfully, did not make the short list? Have these impacted your choices or relationships?

How do your values impact decisions about spending money? *(For example: your top value is curiosity. You have no qualms about spending money on traveling, but balk at the idea of purchasing a video game console).*

Brainstorm ways that you could adjust some logistics to more clearly support your children's values.
(For example: if you have to choose between two things you spend money on, is there a way to adjust spending to support what your child is telling you is important to them?)

How do your values impact other family decisions?

How do your children's interests seem to reflect their values?
(For example: your child says they value "creativity." In what ways do their chosen interests bring out or support creativity?)

Elaborate on this last question. Look through their eyes and think about how they are living a life congruent with their stated values.

MOST CHILDREN DO NOT WANT to spend money on something because they lack values or have negative intentions. When an adult believes that, they are often superimposing their baggage onto their child's money-spending request.

One way to better support and connect with your kids is to look at their money requests and assume good intentions.

Have conversations with your kids about the choices the adults are making with the money. Factor your kids' desires into those choices. Talk about what happens when money goes to column A, and how that means there is less for column B. Talk about why those things are important to you. Ask your children what is important to them to spend money on.

Here is a secret that I have discovered after watching thousands of families in action; saying "no" to your children's requests doesn't teach them frugality or thoughtfulness. It teaches them desperation, which leads to stinginess. Saying "yes" as much and whenever you can, shows your kid over and over that you value them, their likes, and their wants. It shows them that you are on their team and will provide abundantly for them whenever you can. When you can't, they know deep down in their bones that you would say yes if you could. Those kids are understanding. Those kids think creatively about other ways to get what they want. They might be disappointed that they can't have that thing or take that class, but they do not blame the parents or hold on to resentment.

Most people can't say yes to everything that a child wants when it costs money. But most parents can do a few things to increase that number. And you ought to try to increase that number. Abundance in us fosters generosity in them.

Try to cut back on how often you need to say no. If you can avoid taking kids to places where things are too expensive for your budget, excellent. Take them to places where you can say yes more often, such as dollar stores and garage sales.

Buy things they will like when they are on sale and save them for a time you know they will want something. For example, you might buy a package of 12 Hatchimals because they are cheaper than two at a time, stash most of them, and give one each time they ask.

Talk about expectations ahead of time, focusing on what you can do. I can't get something in the toy aisle at Target every time we go, but I can get them something from the dollar bins! We talk excitedly about what there might be in those bins before we get there. If there are two neat things to choose from, we discuss and weigh the benefits of each item before deciding.

Take your kids seriously when they say they like something. Don't huff, sigh, roll your eyes, or call anything "junk." Look at what caught their eye. Sure, maybe it's effective marketing and placement, but still, it caught their eye for a reason. Spend a few moments and say, "Oh yeah! That does look like fun!" Sometimes that's all they need; validation that they saw something interesting.

Take photos and make lists. If you can't get something right away, assure your child you won't forget about it.

Where else are you spending money? I don't think parents need to sacrifice everything for their kids. But, on the other hand, you invited them here. Take joy in their joy.

If it feels like the stuff they want to spend money on is in direct opposition to your values, remember that these moments are opportunities to either build connections or build a wall between you. Choose connection. Be curious about their motivations. If it feels like spending money in their way detracts from big-picture family plans and values, then it's conversation time. And it's time to be realistic about what a child can do. You might be able to decrease your impulse purchases because you know you are planning a family vacation next year and you want to budget for it. Saving up for a year to travel is not a realistic expectation for a seven-year-old (or a 14-year-old, or many 25-year-olds). There will have to be a balance.

Sometimes, it isn't about physical items. Sometimes, a child's interest is just plain expensive! The older they get and the more skilled they become, the cost tends to increase accordingly, but you can still think creatively and find solutions. Use interest-based experiences to satisfy your desire for travel or family time—don't think it has to be two separate events. For example, if your child desperately wants to ride horses, make your next family vacation destination a ranch.

Find ways for you or your interested child to work or volunteer in the field in order to cut down on costs. I know a large number of teens who work in stables to be around horses, apprentice with experts, or work reception desks or maintenance to earn studio time. Some do photography, marketing, blogging, or social media in exchange for space or time. Teaching beginners in their area of interest is a time-honored tradition. And maybe it's not all on the kid; you can take on some of that burden as well. I do the social media for our Kung Fu studio in exchange for my kid's lessons.

Often there are cheaper ways to pursue an interest. Look into city recreation programs, co-ops, or partnering with students who would like more teaching/leading time.

I cannot write about every possibility here. So much depends on your kid, their interests, and your circumstances. What I do know is that desperation and criticism are death to brainstorming, and brainstorming is what is required for creative solutions. Start by being on your kids' side, with the understanding deep down that you are going to do everything you can to get them all the things they want. Start there, and solutions will follow.

Your kids are not bad or selfish for wanting things or for wanting to spend money on those things. They *are* self-centered. They're supposed to be—in the best, most essential way. They center themselves first because it is developmentally impossible to do otherwise and still learn the things they need to learn as humans. Don't hold that against them.

A Note about Values

There is a reason I chose money as the first barrier to explore—the exercise of prioritizing your values will come up again and again. Our values system impacts not only where we choose to spend (or not spend) our money, but also where we choose to spend our time, our energy, and our other resources. It informs how we feel about asking for or accepting help, our attitude towards our children's behaviors, and our messages about what is "normal." Our values reflect what we find scary, and how we define success. Asking you to delve deeply into your patterns and preferences is an on-going values exercise. Each of these barriers will highlight your values-based choices in a different way. It is my hope that you will also be able to see your children's values play out across different realms throughout their lives, rather than feeling like they don't live up to your values, full stop. This values exercise is essential to our work.

BARRIER 2: AGAINST US

Sometimes, the interests our children find and latch onto go very much against our lifestyle, our values, or even our philosophical outlook. I have seen vegetarian parents with intensely carnivorous children who embrace all things bacon. I have seen pacifist parents taken aback by the enthusiasm their child expresses for violent and gory video games. It can be difficult to embrace your child's interests when they seem to be in radical opposition to what you hold dear.

Exercise 7a

Take a moment to list 5-10 roles, or things about your identity, that are important to you.

For example, I am...
...an Artist
...vegetarian
...a teacher
...a Californian

Now list 5-10 traits that are important to you.

For example, I am...
...productive
...organized
...hospitable and people feel cozy at my house
...peaceful and calm
...an explorer, I travel, I like to expose myself to new things
...focused on health and fitness

I THINK it is essential to stop and take stock of the things we value—in general, and about ourselves, specifically. When our children's interests seem to be at odds with what we see as an integral part of our own identity, it can be tough to reconcile. You can resent your children without even realizing that's what is happening. I've seen parents express dislike toward their child because the child's choices seemed in direct opposition to what they valued as "good" or "worthwhile."

If you see yourself as productive, hard-working, consistent, determined, and driven, and you look at your child and see the opposite, it can be challenging to value how they choose to spend their time. It takes work to exercise a different set of muscles; the ones that seek to recognize the value in what they are doing, even if it is different from what you'd choose.

Try hard not to hold anything above your children. Meaning, if you need to put values in a hierarchy, place your kids on the top tier. Everything else is secondary. Everything. Else. Is. Secondary. Take a deep breath. That said, this doesn't mean abandoning everything you hold sacred.

Exercise 7b

Go back to that list of roles. Is "parent to _____[your child's name]" at the top of that list? If it isn't, write it there now.

What are some of the qualities that make you the perfect parent for your child? Maybe things like patience, a willingness to experiment, enthusiasm, the ability not to be grossed out by bugs, or being a good researcher. Make a new list of these valuable traits and characteristics. It is good to remind yourself of them!

As _____'s parent, I am...

WHEN YOU PUT your child at the top of your list, and when you remember to value your parent-related characteristics, it doesn't mean you are giving up everything that makes you unique. You're adding to the list, not erasing from it. You're increasing the range of your flashlight to encompass a broader viewpoint.

It doesn't mean that your children will likewise toss your values in the trash. It means trusting that your example will be enough to impart what you think is important, and that you've instilled enough of your core values to trust their choices. It is developmentally appropriate for kids to push off from their parents, like learning to swim and pushing off the wall of a swimming pool. They will push off from you, regardless of your attitude about their independence. If you can expect it, welcome it, and encourage it, they will swim back around to tell you about their insights and adventures. They will let you be a part of that process. If you hold them, resist their pushing away, and criticize them, it will be weighty. It makes their task harder, it makes them resent you for that hardship, and it decreases the likelihood that they will open up and share what is important to them with you. You cut off that connection.

It is more important that your children have strength of conviction in their own values than that they imitate yours. Even if yours are the best.

Back to the example of the vegetarian pacifist parents. Those kids need to differentiate themselves to accomplish their psychosocial task. It isn't personal. Be curious about them and their thoughts. Don't have an ulterior motive. They'll know. Stay playful and expansive. They aren't espousing values of violence or cruelty, rather they are experimenting with identity, independence, freedom, and choice. Make it a joyful, safe experience and, like Little Bo Peep's sheep, they will come back to you.

And the stories they'll have! The connections they'll make! Differing values aren't something to grit your teeth and tolerate. These moments can be the most dynamic, exciting, love-filled parts of their childhood! The idea that teens are difficult and resistant is pervasive and an absolute myth. Support them and protect their passions. Learn to speak their love language. Connect with courage. You will be so happy and amazed.

Exercise 7c

Is there a positive way your child has surprised you with their interest? A piece of knowledge you didn't realize they had discovered? A skill they have honed that is amazing? Write about that.

BARRIER 3: RISK

Sometimes it is difficult to support our children's interests because they scare the living daylights out of us. They have dangerous and risky interests. I want to talk a bit about risk. Our goal as parents should not be to eliminate all risk! We miss out on crucial shaping and development if we do that. We inhibit our children's abilities and growth. Our goal should be to help our children as they confidently increase their skill levels to be able to handle risk without lasting negative consequences.

Let's tackle a few logistical questions, and then move on to the benefits of risk.

Push the pause button on your emotional side for a minute and pretend you are looking at someone else's child. Is their activity genuinely dangerous? Is there a high likelihood that they will get injured? In the recreation field, we use this handy little risk management grid:

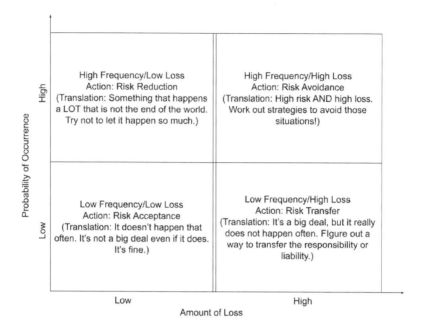

The idea being, if it's low potential damage and low frequency, we don't need to address it. If it's high stakes and low frequency, then we probably don't need to do anything except have an emergency plan or protocol in place. If it's high potential damage *and* high frequency, then we need to take it seriously and change something about it.

So, in the case of your kid's activity, is it high danger with a high chance that the risk will happen? If the answer is truly, objectively, *yes*, then is there a way to adapt the activity without losing its integrity? Maybe new or better equipment? Maybe a more effective space? Maybe more skilled mentors? Maybe more practice, not less? If you get high-quality resources, will that help minimize the risk and protect their passion and your relationship?

On the rare occasion that their interest will absolutely intersect with certain harm and there is nothing to be done about it, I hope that you have built a long history of supporting your child. Because the children who can trust that their parents have their back and *want* to help them are the ones who understand that when you say, "I'm so sorry, this just can't be done," you are speaking the truth. They are forgiving. They are understanding. They may be disappointed, but it is usually not targeted at the parent. That is one of the wonderful side effects of being on their team rather than having a history of adversity. They will trust you! If this has not been the case for you, you can start now. Make your next choice a truthful, supportive one. Then the next one after that. Don't be mean and create lessons. Connect with them and be their teammate. Try very hard to get them the things that will aid them in their interest. Try to minimize the risk instead of deciding they can have nothing more to do with it. Try to be creative and resourceful about the barriers first.

Notice I said minimize risk, not eliminate it. Again, our goal is not to eliminate all risk because there are measurable and important benefits to it.

I remember being six years old, playing in our front yard with the neighbors, feeling like I owned the whole universe. I remember the deep exploration behind bushes and trees, and the "tiny infinities" that exist when children have the time to delve into their play. I remember the exciting rush of adrenaline when we would swing from a branch, the slower burn of nervousness when we would venture further and further from my house and go to other neighbors' yards. My world felt vast; it felt like freedom.

One day, expressing this feeling to my mom, she laughed and laughed. Gratified, she told me that she tried hard to make it feel that way, but in actuality she or a neighbor always had their eyes on us. She was watching, learning our tendencies and letting us figure things out. We dealt with conflict, injured birds, ant bites, taking turns to ride the bike, and hurt feelings. She helped when we asked, and she paid attention.

Her control over our safety was like a fence around the yard. When we wanted to expand our reach and she knew we were capable, she'd expand the (metaphorical) fence, just before we even knew it was there. So, for us, we never hit that border; there was no barrier or resistance.

She was active in this process, like a theater technician behind the scenes making the show on stage look like effortless magic. Another great example of this was when I got a little older and wanted to travel more. My parents made it a point to take our family on trips, engaging me in the planning and problem-solving process so that they could give me as much experience in relative safety as possible before that perimeter fence expanded again.

Because here's the thing: We want growth for our children. We all know adults whose development seems stalled, who seem to wrap the status quo around them like a weighted security blanket. We know people who hold on tightly to the old version of who they are, refusing to let new experiences or information shape them. That is not healthy, and we want our kids to be healthy. Growth doesn't happen in perfect comfort.

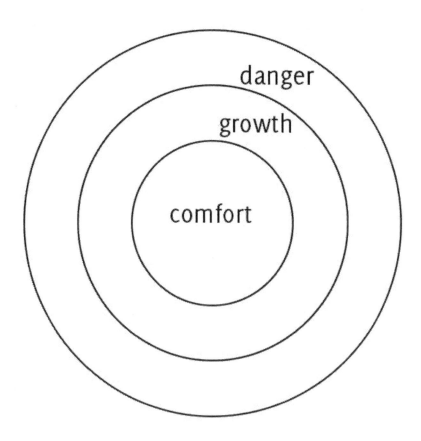

Consider these three concentric circles, with comfort at the center. Good things can totally happen in that comfy center place! Rest and recovery, for example. Both are valuable, giving us the space to process and revitalize ourselves for a time when we are ready to expand, which then leads to growth. Over and over again, nature shows us examples of how growth can sometimes be downright painful. My favorite is Sequoia trees which literally need fire for new shoots to sprout. There are eggs, which crack, and cocoons that shred; growth is painful but necessary. We try to give our kids the knowledge and certainty that they have what it takes to handle discomfort and pain. We create for them a story in which they are the protagonist and fairy godparent all in one, but we can't teach every dragon-fighting technique because we don't yet know the dragons they will encounter. We *can* ensure that they trust that they have or can learn the skills they will need when their dragons appear.

The neat thing about growth zones is that they change. Once you've been in a place for a while, the newness wears off and it becomes familiar and comforting. The comfort zone is a big warm gooey blob that keeps loyally following at our heels as we wander and expand.

Exercise 8

Draw and fill in the concentric circles.

- In the inner circle, list the specific interests your children have that you have no trouble supporting and enjoying.
- In the middle circle list those that cause you stress and that you have some resistance to but can imagine the possibility of supporting more fully.
- In the third circle, list the interests they have (or could have) that make you want to lock them in their rooms and wrap them in bubble wrap.

Take a few moments and write about these activities and interests. What comes to mind?

Organize your list into three columns: comfort zone, growth zone, and danger zone.

Do you see any themes between the activities/interests you've listed in each zone? Over and over again I ask parents, "What are you afraid of?" These lists can be a good place to start.

For example, many parents list things like the following:

Comfort Zone
Activities:
Soccer
Guitar
Reading
Piano
Dance

Themes:
Active
Exercise
Teams
Learning

Growth Zone
Activities:
Video games
Hockey
Horseback riding
Racing

Themes:
Scary

Risky
Costs a lot of money
Needs a lot of equipment
Would be fine if they were older/bigger
Too intense

Danger Zone
Activities:
Gambling
Extreme sports
YouTube
Internet-based

Themes:
Passive
Time-suck
Weird
Stranger-danger
Unhealthy
Addictive
Physically dangerous

I OFTEN TELL my clients that our fears and past experiences (which lead to some of our worries) are like boxes and trunks and old furniture; we gather them over time and through circumstance and toss them into a big, dark, internal basement. We are in total darkness, bumping into things, and it hurts; we scrape our shins and stub our toes over and over again in the dark.

Self-exploration, whether through therapy or a book like this, is like being handed a flashlight. We point our beam of light at those large, impassive, frightening objects that are cluttering our mental and emotional space and take a hard look. We sift through piles of baggage. We decide, consciously, to let some things go. Others we stack up neater and decide they might be useful to us. The result is less pain and much more awareness.

Your fears relating to your children's interests are not just about the specific activity. They are bigger than that. They are connected to those mysterious shapes in your inner basement in need of a good airing out. Without exploring these, you are making decisions based on fear. You are letting piles of unchecked pain impact your children's connections, learning, self-worth, and future.

Sure, some things are flat out dangerous no matter what sort of light you shine on them. In my experience, however, there are fewer of these than we think and in some cases the risks can be mitigated with *more* support for the activity, rather than less. Most children, when controlled or restricted, are experts at finding workarounds to the rules. Don't let your fears and anxieties create a relationship with your children where they must sneak to do the risky behavior. Instead, help them find safer ways to experience their interests.

Sometimes you can change your perspective about the very idea of risk and danger. Studies show that kids experience fewer injuries on "adventure-style" playgrounds than the mass-produced-for-safety play equipment you tend to see at schools. These "adventure" playgrounds often have heights, loose and rickety parts, tools and rusty nails, handmade zip lines, big pieces of old metal, and lots of ways children could get hurt, yet we see fewer injuries!

One big reason for this is that there usually isn't a clearly defined "one right way" to use the equipment at an adventure playground. This means that kids with varying levels of reach and coordination can use it in a variety of ways that better fit their skill and ability levels. And because there tends to be many ways to use the equipment, they encourage more learning opportunities through different combinations of balance, strength, stamina, and coordination. This translates to kids who are more skilled at physical play. They are better able to assess the risks or skill necessary to complete a physical task, weigh their own abilities accordingly, find creative workarounds to barriers, gain more confidence/skill incrementally, and keep up in creative ways with more "advanced" friends, diminishing any shame and embarrassment of potentially falling behind or "doing it wrong."

The same is true for other types of play and unorthodox or "risky" interest areas. The skills needed might not be forearm muscle strength, but the principle is the same, even when what is required is emotional intelligence, conflict management, or assertiveness. Perceived risk is important because it is what puts us in the growth zone. I say perceived risk for a reason; if dry sand is comfortable and the deep ocean is dangerous, the place where water meets shore is growth.

Have you ever watched a toddler play in that wet-sand space? They watch, run, squeal, jump back to the dry sand, and run forward to meet the water. There is adrenaline, excitement, and some very real fear. Ideally, there is a parent nearby, smiling and clapping, holding hands if their child wants to test their courage in a few more inches of water. That's the perceived part: you're letting them feel the risk without being in real danger. Kids who get thrown into the deep end, or the danger zone, might learn how to swim, but they also learn other things, like how that adult isn't safe, can't be trusted, and that it isn't safe to stick a toe out of their comfort zone. Kids who venture out on their own, free of judgement if they need to retreat to safety, build a foundation of trust and security. Trusting, secure kids turn into trusting, secure adults.

So, provide an expanding fence, a safe place on dry sand, and be willing to wade out to them when the growth is painful. Leave the nt. Help them take risks. Comfort them when it's hard.

beach is a metaphor. It will look different when they are six, , or eighteen. Work on visualizing a gorgeous shoreline and y toddler days, so that you can treat their next experiment and erest in the same way.

Sometimes, their activities don't always have the best results. Sometimes, they will break things or get hurt. A concerned mother in a group I was in once asked about what to do when the consequence of their children's actions led to actual physical damage.

This was my response:

If I was so [angry, invested, emotional on any level] that I did property damage or broke something, how would I want to be treated?

I think I'd want my [husband, parent, the adult] to help make the next part easier for me, because obviously I am going through something really difficult.

I think it would be a show of amazing love and kindness if he got the materials to fix it, and while doing so, gave me smiles and smooches and was extra kind to me.

I would probably join in fixing, and if he didn't try to impart some sort of lesson, I might feel safe enough to start talking about what was upsetting me to begin with, or express remorse that my feelings led to breaking something.

I'd like for him to say, a lot, "It's okay, I understand."

That, I think, would show love, create connection, and model a way of handling emotions that I want to emulate.

Remember that what you believe you are teaching isn't always what is conveyed or internalized. A lot of mental health issues stem from feeling that we are not worthy of love—that love is conditional and must be earned.

If a parent punishes their child in this scenario, the message sent is: "I will only be loving towards you if you are not upset/angry." That "if" is important; it sets the condition. If a parent requires their kid to pay for and immediately fix that [wall, table, controller, toy...], there is some element of imparting the idea that "This [wall, table, controller, toy...] is more important than your feelings." It might not be what the parent intends, but impact is different than intent. Take a minute and choose unconditional love and compassion. Other lessons can wait.

BARRIER 4: TIME

A few things come up when we talk about time:

- We don't have time for that.
- If they spend time doing *this*, they won't do other (more) important things.
- This is a waste of time and won't lead to success later.
- Their interest requires too much time.
- There isn't enough time to do it all.
- It would be okay if it took up less time.

Exercise 9

Does something come to mind that you could add to that list? W· ˙
down.

Time is a loaded topic. Take it from a ɴ·
studies field; people hold a lot ᴏᶠ˙
and the immorality of wasᵗ˙
watch their children "·

the older we are, the faster time seems to go. There's an element of wishing we could go back to when we were younger and use our time differently. It's not fair, though, to project our regretful hindsight onto our kids.

If you find yourself saying things like, "All they want to do is That Thing," I want you to make a list of their activities over the past week. Think about all the different things they did, including things like classes, activities, park days, playgroups, lessons, trips to grocery stores, restaurants, friends' houses, walking the dog, playgrounds, throwing a ball outside, reading a book, making dinner etc. *Include it all.* If you're going to have feelings about the quantity of time spent on an activity, you should have a realistic idea of how much time that actually is first.

Now let's look at a single day by filling in a pie chart – draw a big circle and divide it into 24 segments, with each segment representing one hour of the day. What have they actually spent their time doing? *Be specific.*

Do they get up to use the restroom? When have they slept? Had food? How long have they been focused on this activity? One week? Six months? Really, how long?

Time for some statistics. What do you think the realistic probability would be that that worst-case scenario will happen? Is it 100% likely to happen? 75%? 25%? 10%? Based on that probability, how much do you want your behavior, thoughts, and feelings driven by your fear of it happening?

Whose voice do you hear in your head as you contemplate your worst fear about how your kid spends their time? Most of us have a "we should behave this way because..." voice that comes from someone close to us as we were growing up. Who is yours?

Is this a person you want to emulate in this way?

What was your relationship like with that person?

Is your relationship with them something you want to repeat with your child?

How did you learn about how you should spend your time? There are many sayings and idioms related to time. "Idle hands are the devil's playthings," for instance. What are some things you were taught to believe about how you should spend free time?

Are there more ways you can facilitate your child's passion? Can you give them the gift of even more time?

Take the next few questions as an opportunity to dig in and explore you and your family's values as they relate to time, work, leisure, and choice.

Did you feel like you had lots of free time as a kid?

Was there an age where that changed? How old were you? What were the circumstances?

How did you feel about it then? How do you feel about it now?

Did you see the important adults in your life engaging in play?

Did they have free time?

Who did the bulk of household work? Did they have free time?

Who did the bulk of money-making work? Did they have free time?

Did they ever share their philosophy or beliefs about work?

If you had to summarize their attitude towards play, what would it be?

Did any family members have common idioms or sayings about time?

As a kid, what did your daily schedule look like?

What about when you were a teenager?

What about when you lived away from your family of origin?

When was the last time you felt like you had discretionary time?

Do you ever experience guilt about how you spend your time?

If you could go back in time and give advice to your younger self, what would it be?

Do you believe there is value in time spent without a greater purpose?

Did you take vacations when you were young?

Do you take vacations now?

If you suddenly were gifted 36 hours in every day, what would you do with your extra time?

What do you do in your free time now?

What would you like to do?

Why don't you have more free time?

How do you want your kid to spend their time?

LET'S go back to that first list of common issues parents bring up in regards to their kids' interests and time.

"We don't have time for that."

My first questions to a parent who says this are: Why? What are you doing instead? Is that other thing truly a necessity? Who decided? When was the last time you negotiated? Are there creative ways you could do more things?

Time is so subjective. Every semester, I ask my students to track their time for one week and discuss their insights. Remember that you and your child are probably not viewing time in the same way at all. Try to imagine time from their perspective. Try to create a sense of abundance for them in this way as well.

"If they spend time doing this, they won't do other important things."

Every minute of your life is a choice—not between two things, but between *all* the things. Every minute they spend doing this thing is one they spend not doing everything else; an infinite number of other options. Here's your job as a parent: see that fact as comforting rather than terrifying. Let it open your mind because looking at time as if there are only two choices is narrow and unhelpful. So yes, the reality is that they won't do other important things if they are doing this thing. They also won't be doing other terrible things if they are doing this thing. Perspective switch! Also, take a second to consider that this thing is important to them.

Take some time to think about and write down why this activity is important to your child.

"It is a waste of time and won't lead to success later."

Stop. No, it is not, I promise. I absolutely promise you, as a professional, that it is not a waste of time. Because here's the thing, you have no idea what this experience could connect to in the future. Those teachers who said we wouldn't have calculators in our pockets? They are probably feeling quite silly now. We don't know the skills, traits, or tools that will best serve our children in the future, so you genuinely cannot judge whether or not it is a waste of time in the present.

If they are choosing to do this thing in their discretionary time then that means they inherently find value in it, and if they find value in it, then it is not a waste. Look for the value.

Define success for yourself and for your kid right now.

How will you know when you have reached success?

What other ways are there to measure success?

"Their interest requires too much time."

It requires too much time for whom? You or them? If it is you, this is a valid concern to address creatively. It's possible that their interest is incredibly demanding and requires sacrifice or a lot of problem-solving and dedication. Is this a gift you can give your kid? Or are you feeling resentful? Very often the parents I talk to who have issues with the amount of time their kids are spending on something are feeling time deprived in other ways that can be addressed separately rather than projected onto their kids. It's also possible that parents have other kids and many other activities to manage and are having a hard time feeling like they can do it all. That is a real issue to deal with, but not one that your kid necessarily needs to be a part of.

Sometimes parents think that the time their kid is spending on that one activity is "too much" because they get uncomfortable when people do anything intensely or passionately. The message that your kid is "too much" can be a damaging one, so try to be wary of even thinking that way. Everyone deserves time to explore. Your kids deserve vast expanses of time to dive into the things that bring them intrinsic satisfaction.

Yes, spending that kind of time in one area means they are not doing other things. It is only your perspective of loss that makes that seem like a negative thing. When parents say, "But it takes too much time away from other things," I want to know what the specifics are. They are usually things like school work or chores. Given what we know about how we learn, kids are learning in a much more valuable way when they have the freedom to dive into something for hours and hours rather than feeling forced into doing an arbitrary (to them) assignment given to them by someone else. Time isn't wasted—what they learn in one area transfers to another. Playing video games increases hand-eye coordination, and it's not like that disappears when they put down the controller. Dedication, commitment, expertise, follow-through, investment—these are the words that prospective employers use to describe who they want to hire. Problem-solvers, curious, innovators—these are the traits that college admission officers use to describe the students they want attending their schools. We learn these traits through a combination of time and choice.

Are there ways to restructure those other things, for now?

Many parents are worried about time spent in seemingly unhealthy ways, with eyes close to screens and spines succumbing to poor posture. We worry that they are not looking lively and engaged. First, remember that a screen is a portal to incredible things; just because we may not know what they're getting out of it, does not mean they aren't. Second, have you watched yourself read a book? How lively and engaged do you look? I think that is a good litmus test whenever you are worried about how they're spending their time. Would you have the same fear if they were spending those hours with a book? Would you have the same concern if they were spending hours knitting? Building with Lego? Watching bugs outside? The answer is usually no, which means it is not as much about time as it is about fear of a particular activity.

We ask so much of children. Some schools start at 7 am and go until 3 pm—kids who are in daycare start before that and stay after. Kids are attending more recreational programming than they ever have before. The number of hours of homework has increased. Kids in school and programmed activities spend most of their time around other people and all of their noise and demands. Their time is tightly scheduled and dictated by bells and alarms. How do you feel after a day like that? Give them the gift of time and autonomy when it is available to them.

"There isn't enough time to do it all."

No, there isn't. One of the essential things to remember is that you don't *need* to do it all. First, do like doctors do, and check if you are doing harm or standing in their way. My child loves martial arts. At this point, I am not equipped to set up an entire martial arts studio in our garage (although that certainly might be an awesome creative solution to a different problem!). But I can facilitate his involvement in a supportive martial arts studio near us. It is not the closest martial arts studio. Sometimes it is inconvenient to get him there two or three times a week for class and belt tests. It also means other involvement, like parties and fundraisers. But when I watch his eyes light up, when I see him practicing his lessons, when I watch how seriously they listen to his opinion, and when I hear about how those skills helped him through a difficulty, I'm glad we made it happen. I'm reminded that sometimes it's better when our kids learn things from other people. My job, in this case, is to make sure his uniform is clean and ready to go, that I have enough gas in the car, that he has had access to food beforehand, and that I make sure we leave on time. It isn't my job to be a professional-level Kung Fu instructor or to have a facility with mats, bags, and weapons. Instead, I facilitate.

It's time to start looking at creative solutions. Are there ways to get other people to help?

"It would be okay if it took up less time."

That sounds like you're pretending to be giving and generous, but when we look closer it is a values statement about the amount of worth you give that activity. "Your interest is worth thirty minutes but not sixty," for example. What message is that sending to your kid about their ability to make decisions, determine value, and learn about themselves? We don't get to decide how much time an interest is worth to someone else.

BARRIER 5: SPACE

My background is in recreation and leisure studies. There was a time when I was working towards becoming a recreation therapist. One of the key tenets of therapeutic recreation is to help patients hold on to the fidelity of their activity of choice while making the necessary adaptations to make it logistically workable for their circumstances. For example, if I loved to snowboard, I might first sit with a recreation therapist and think about what it was I got out of that activity. Perhaps for me, the main point was the adrenaline rush. Maybe it was being outside in the snow and the sunshine. Maybe it was the snowboarding culture, the escape to nature, or the friends I met up with at the hill.

The point is to keep asking, "Why, why, why?" Once you discover what the core benefits and satisfactions of the activity are, keep hold of those as you make adaptations. Perhaps they can't stand up to snowboard anymore, so they use adaptive equipment to maintain the adrenaline rush of flying down a mountain. Maybe they realize it was about escaping to the mountains, so you choose to do that in another way, adapting the experience rather than sticking to that specific sport. You hold on to the core of it, whatever that may be for *you*.

When people come to my office and say, "I'd like to support my kid in this, but our house is too small/we have no backyard/there are three kids in one room/we don't have storage for the supplies," one of the things I ask them to do is stop and think about what the core benefit is for their child. When your kid develops an interest in something, you immediately imagine what that looks like. When I say, "hockey," most of us think of a rink with ice. When I say "oil painting," there are easels and paint brushes involved. True, your first thought about the set up might not be doable, but, like a recreation therapist, take a minute to explore with your child what possible adaptations could be made to provide space for the core of their interest to shine through.

I recognize that space is a privilege. Some of you reading this will have ample square footage to play with creatively. Others will have a borrowed room in someone else's place. I've seen creative solutions in every sized setting.

There is more than one way to set up a space to support your kid.

Part of this involves thinking creatively and being willing to try something, see if it works, and make adjustments if necessary. Try not to think of the first thing you try as a permanent solution.

Part of this involves looking at your life realistically, rather than expectantly. Do you have a large dining room table, placed there with hopes of nightly family dinner and gameplay? Do you use it that way? Does it get used once a year? What might your actual not-nightly-monopoly-playing family use that space for instead? Let go of the pretty picture and look at your real family.

Part of this involves looking at your space as *space* rather than as the function everyone else uses it as. A flower bed doesn't need to hold flowers. A bedroom doesn't need to have a bed. Maybe there are unique ways to use your space you haven't thought of yet. Many families who are successful in this department divide up their family space based on functionality. Rather than individual bedrooms, there is a room for sleeping and clothes, a room for computer stuff, or a room for toys and supplies. Your family and thus your living space, will be unique to you. Try to see past "how it has always been" or societal expectations. Be curious about what could work! Think of it as a challenge, a game.

Part of this involves understanding what they really want. Does your kid want to practice certain skills? Or is it more important to them to be surrounded by the things they love? A full ice hockey rink in your yard? To this southern Californian, that sounds super difficult. But setting up a smaller space to practice shooting a puck into a net? Maybe that can happen. Maybe it would be enough for you to make a wall with photos of their favorite hockey players. Maybe it would be enough to put hockey-related supplies in an easy-to-reach tub for occasional use. What would feel supportive *to your kid*? What do they want?

A woman came asking for help. Her daughter had repeatedly been asking for "her own space," and the mom had immediately gone to, "there are four kids in one room, we just don't have the space—there is no solution!" She was preemptively distraught. Her child knew the situation, and it felt like a personal jab at her for her daughter to be asking for this impossible request. I asked, "What kind of space does she want?" The mom couldn't answer right away. She realized she had gone straight to feeling defeated and hadn't even stopped to explore with her kid. She reported back a little later that it was a combination of things. Her kid wanted a space she could decorate, and she didn't like seeing her siblings' lights on when she was trying to fall asleep at night. With this information, we had ideas. She ended up moving that daughter's bed to the corner, so she had two walls, and then used PVC pipe to create a frame she could hang curtains around. Her daughter was able to decorate with cloth, pin-up pictures, and close the curtains around her at night for her own space. She was thrilled. Turns out, they had the space for that after all.

SOME OF THIS involves being solution-oriented and asking for help. Get your kid involved with finding solutions. If you are genuinely yes-oriented, if your kid knows you are looking for a way to support them, and you tell them honestly about the barriers, they might have some good ideas. Ask around. What have other parents done? What have professionals in that activity done? Look for inspiration! Look at museum exhibits or library displays.

Some of this involves thinking about time. Perhaps it isn't feasible that each kid gets a dedicated space for their interest, but maybe you could try something for a week or a month, and then change it again.

Some of this involves self-esteem and security. Let's say you re-arrange your side-yard into a scooter-skateboard-rollerblade-unicycle repair shop. Or you get rid of your dining room table and turn the space into Lego storage. Or half of your kitchen becomes a robotics-slime-art-museum-studio-factory-lab. When a friend or neighbor comes to visit and expresses their surprise, instead of feeling defensive, work towards being able to smile, knowing with a calm certainty that you're supporting your kids and doing what is right for your family. Most of the time, you don't need to respond or justify. It is enough to know that you are protecting their passions.

Some of this involves looking outside of your living space. Do you have public spaces near you that could feel like theirs? Do they go somewhere for lessons or studio time related to their interest that can feel like a second home? I had a corner of a library that felt like my special spot when I was little. When I was older, a college ceramic studio saw more of me than my bedroom did. Establishing that feeling requires a different set of resources (like an ability and willingness to get there frequently). Still, sometimes we have more of one resource than another, and this might be a possibility.

Part of this involves looking at your values around using space in the same way you looked at your values around spending money. What are you saying about who and what you value, based on what is receiving space?

There usually isn't just one magical solution. Figuring out a way to provide a supportive space for your child's interest is a big game of trial and error, picking from different creative solutions to explore what works for you and yours.

Exercise 10

Here are some questions to help you play!

Are there any underutilized spaces in your home?

If you were to ask your kid what their dream space looked like, what would they say?

List three ways you could incorporate some elements of your kid's dream space into your current living situation.

Where does your kid spend most of their time right now?

Why do you think they gravitate towards that place?

What kind of storage would be ideal for the supplies or equipment for their interest?

Where is their favorite place to be outside of their home? What is it about that place that makes it so inviting?

What are some ways you could bring any of those elements into your home?

If you were to write a mission statement for your home, like a business writes a mission statement, what would it include? What is your home's purpose?

How is space divvied up right now?

How are decisions made about your space?

When someone unrelated to you comes to your home, what impression do you want them to have?

Did you have any special spaces outside of your home when you were younger? What were they like? What made them special? What made them possible?

Did you have your own space in your home growing up?

If a stranger had walked into your home when you were a child, would they have known what you were interested in?

How were decisions made about space in your family when you were a child?

Do you and your partner share values regarding space and use? Are there conflicts? What do they typically center on?

Write your thoughts regarding equality and fairness when it comes to the space in your home. Is it important that everyone has equal space? Why or why not?

BARRIER 6: NO RESOURCES NEAR US

B e vocal about your children's interests for the simple reason that you never know who might know someone who may be able to help. When you join a group or are waiting in line at the grocery store, don't let opportunities pass you by to talk about your children's hopes and dreams. If someone gives you a lead, follow up on it.

I've seen some emotional hang-ups that can prevent parents from doing this. Things like feeling they need to do it all themselves, that they would be imposing on others, a strong desire to be independent, or feeling unworthy of accepting offers of help. Recognize if you have any issues in these areas, and don't let them impact your children's access to supportive people or spaces.

In my experience, most people love sharing their interests with other interested people. If you feel like you are imposing, do a check of the evidence:

- Have they made a negative comment about the amount of time or effort it takes to involve you or your kid?
- Have they invited you and your child back?
- Have they used words that describe excitement,

enjoyment, or pleasure at sharing resources with your child?

- Have they expended considerable resources, and have you thanked them or reciprocated in some way?

What are some reasons you might be feeling like you are imposing? Are you unused to generosity? Do you feel like you need to give back with an equal gesture? Have your relationships always been transactional?

It is common in social media, mainstream parenting blogs, and television and movies to act like parents should not be inconvenienced by their children. I want to officially, formally, and professionally, give you permission to go above and beyond for your children. It is okay to do big things for them. It is okay to plan entire family vacations around their interests. It is okay to load up the car and drive across the country to see or do something they want to do. It won't "spoil" them. It won't be a waste. It won't mean they "run your household" or that you "have no control." I have dozens of wonderful stories from parents who have facilitated extreme and amazing experiences for their kids—including driving thirty hours to get somewhere, overcoming serious phobias, launching businesses, and international travel.

I have not yet heard any regrets.

BARRIER 7: OTHER FAMILY MEMBERS HAVE NEEDS TOO

I t can add to the challenge when you are the parent of several children who all have needs. Sometimes even at the same time! Here are a few ways you might be able to work through feelings of being overwhelmed, stretched too thin, and the resentment that can be born from those feelings so that you can support all of your children.

Remember that while this is how it is right now it will not be this way forever—or even for very long. In the same way that midnight diaper changing felt like it was never going to end, the phase you are in right now is also ephemeral. Take deep breaths and remind yourself of this when you are despairing.

Another valuable point to remember: not everyone needs equal disbursement of the resources at all times. Balance and equality happens over time. We often get it into our heads that each kid needs the exact same thing—whether that's money spent on them, the number of birthday gifts, time with each parent etc. But after a certain point, especially with bigger concept things, kids will understand some differences. They might still want exactly three cookies each when you're handing them out, but the fact that the oldest ends up with half the activities budget for their hockey team while the younger ones split the rest is probably not a big concern for them. Kids' needs change over time. There will be times when each kid soaks up more of the resources, and that's normal. Trying to keep everything exactly even is an exhausting and impossible feat.

Sometimes it does need some conversation with everyone, but kids whose interests are actively supported and who feel a sense of abundance tend to be much more on board helping to support their siblings' interests as well. They are more invested in the happiness of their siblings.

Ask everyone for solutions, including your kids. If everyone knows that their needs are valid and important, they will feel valued and want to contribute toward creative solutions for these logistical tangles.

When you are looking for creative solutions, don't forget your Brainstorming 101 skills. When brainstorming, you are going for an avalanche of outlandish ideas. Quantity leads to quality, and the more off-the-wall, the better. Humor helps us be more creative, and those silly ideas can lead to solutions that will work realistically. The editing process is a separate one from brainstorming.

If your kids are not into figuring out the creative solutions for each other's sake, don't be above bribery. I'm serious about this. You don't have to call it bribery if that's hard for you. When we have to go to work and it's a little unpleasant, it's really nice to get compensated, right? You can show your gratitude with material compensation, like a stop at the ice cream shop on the way home.

Maybe other little logistical shifts could help. If everyone has to go along for Kid 1's soccer practice, you could stop at the library and get new books for Kid 2 along the way. Think ahead and make sure tablets are charged or bring a friend along for an on-the-go playdate.

Use your resources and ask for help. If you're in the mindset of trying to make this work and you are vocal about your needs, it's "preparation for inspiration," as an old professor of mine used to say. Prepare your attitude, ask for help, and be receptive to inspiration from other people's ideas.

BARRIER 8: THEY DON'T WANT US INVOLVED

My responses to this barrier changes depending on the age of your child, but most of the parents I speak to with this challenge have near-teens or teenagers. Most of these relationships have had some damage in this area.

What are some of the reasons your kid wouldn't want you involved in their interest?

- Because you have treated it recklessly in the past.
- Because you have shown disinterest.
- Because you have used it as a punishment.
- Because you have tried to take over.
- Because you aren't expert-level enough and it takes a toll on them to go back to your level.
- Because they don't trust you.
- Because they want something that's all theirs and it has nothing to do with you.

Luckily, with awareness and desire you can work on repairing past damage.

Know when to back off and let it be theirs.

Pay attention and follow their lead. Let them drive. Stick out your thumb, ask for a hitch, but if they'd rather not invite you along for the ride, that could be some solid information about how you might have treated their passions in the past. People tend to protect what they love, so are they protecting their interests from potential judgement or harshness from you? I'm sorry if it hurts. Yet it is better to know and begin repairing the relationship.

Let's do a few lists to work on that repair! Try to do this without badgering them. Be watchful, curious, and positive. This is *your* work to do, not theirs.

Exercise 11

List or find out your kid's favorite:

- Character
- Superhero
- Book
- Movie
- YouTuber
- Video game
- Hogwarts house

Caring about the details shows you care about them.

Do you know how to play their favorite game?

Watch your kid for a while. Take a deep breath and sink below the initial surface panic that they will never do anything else with their life. Let yourself notice the little details of that person that used to be a baby, see their eyelashes and their fingers. Can you remember them younger? That lifting feeling, that expansive feeling, hold on to that while you watch them now.

Write down five things they might be enjoying about their activity.

Write down ten things they might be learning when they're doing their activity.

Write down three connections to something else they might make along the way. Note: This is just an exercise. If they're not interested in pursuing these particular connections, drop it. The idea is to remind you that things can connect in ways we can't predict. For example, my interest in dressing up in costumes led me to wear a bonnet, which led me to Laura Ingalls Wilder, which led me to heritage arts, which led me to knitting, which led me to own a yarn subscription box business.

There are many possible benefits to their chosen activity. Write down at least three for each of these categories: Physical; Cognitive/Mental; Emotional; Social/Relational. And then keep writing as many as you can think of.

Is there anything that would make them more successful in their pursuit of this interest?

- Equipment?
- Space?
- Furniture?
- Atmosphere?

What is *your* favorite game, hobby, type of play?

When is the last time you've done that?

Schedule the next time now.

BARRIER 9: THEY KEEP CHANGING THEIR MINDS

There is a word for this! Your child, my friend, is a dabbler! Girl Scouts, long ago, had badges called "dabbler badges" and they were fantastic. They validated and celebrated kids who were interested in exploring a variety of different things. For example, instead of awarding a badge for, say, learning how to play the trumpet, the "music dabbler badge" might ask girls to experience six or seven different types of instruments or genres of music, or to interview people in a variety of music-related careers. It was a fantastic idea, honoring the fact that exposure to different things is also beneficial.

Kids who jump from topic to topic can often get a bad rap, especially if they do not have insight into their dabbling tendencies. I have known many of these kids, who, for the three weeks they play basketball, live and breathe the court. For the two months of their ceramics interest, they devote their whole life to clay. Four days into fidget spinners they want to spend their (and your) entire life savings on dozens of the things. Dabblers pose their own set of challenges, sure, but the biggest thing to remember is that this can be a powerful skill set.

We often call these kids flaky, inconsistent, or talk about their lack of dedication, concentration, or focus. Stop talking about them like that. They are passionate, curious explorers; intense risk-takers. They are courageous, vulnerable, and open-minded.

There is benefit to dabbling, namely that you get exposed to so many wonderful things! When you jump from topic to topic, you learn about different fields. You meet new people, explore ideas, and get to experience variety. Parents are often worried that without long-term exposure to a single topic, their children will not find a satisfying career or job. First, there are parents who are worried that their kids aren't experiencing enough variety because their children are on their fourth hour of the same activity, so remember that the grass is always greener on the other side. Second, stop worrying about the future and think about what they are getting out of what they are doing *right now*.

Dabblers often report that they would never have been able to predict where they ended up, career-wise, but when they look back, it is easy to see the path. The dots can and do connect. Maybe common themes run through their varied passions that eventually lead to employment. Maybe they will have had so much experience in so many different arenas that they are better able to articulate the type of working environment they prefer. If they do settle to one thing, they may be more certain that it is the right choice for them, precisely because of their range of experience.

BARRIER 10: THEY ARE ONLY INTERESTED IN ONE THING

I hear a lot of parents talk about how their kid wants to watch the same thing over and over. If you feel troubled by that, I would ask if you have ever reread a book, or turned to a favorite movie repeatedly?

Exercise 12

What are some possible reasons a person might want to re-watch a show?

How does my list compare to yours?

- They find it soothing.
- It reminds them of a specific time.
- It creates an atmosphere they want to embrace.
- It provides security or comfort.
- It's fun to know all the lines.
- They can look at the details now—the lighting, the music,

the costume design, the camera angles, the editing, the acting—and take in details that add richness to the experience.

- They can make connections to other types of media.
- It makes them feel a sense of knowledge or mastery, to know something so well.
- It's seasonal or traditional.

WHAT IT REALLY COMES DOWN TO is that they are still getting something out of it. They benefit from re-watching, otherwise they wouldn't be doing it.

So, why is that difficult for parents to watch? If your child watches the same show 25 times in a single day, what are you afraid will happen?

Many parents have a hard time articulating an answer. They have a vague sense that there's something weird or off. They are worried that their kids have lost their sense of control or the ability to choose a different activity. They wonder if it's addicting.

It takes repeated attempts to become good at something. It takes a lot of different ways of experiencing the same thing, over time, to learn a lot about it. I often wish my students understood that integrating information requires more than simply reading the material, but also thinking, talking, and writing about the material. They tend to skim once and think they understand. Realize that when your child is diving deeply into something, they are integrating it into their understanding of the world.

It sometimes seems like kids can't win. If they spend "too much" time on one interest, we worry that they won't be well-rounded or that they are missing out on other experiences; that they are "obsessed" and will stop being able to function. When kids don't stick with one particular interest for very long, we fear they will never find something to pursue, that they are inconsistent, have no follow-through, and will never learn the positives of dedication, engagement or perseverance. Parents stand on both sides, enviously looking at the other patch of green grass.

BARRIER 11: MY SPOUSE ISN'T INTO IT

I am going to add two caveats before I begin this section. First, when I refer to "spouse," I am talking about anyone with whom you are in a committed co-parenting relationship. Second, I am not discussing excessively controlling or abusive relationships. Those two circumstances fall outside the realm of this conversation, and I highly encourage anyone in an unhealthy relationship to seek counseling immediately.

Bonus caveat: I assume that if you are reading this book, your goal is to have better relationships and more harmony in your family overall, not just with your children. If contention with your spouse is a valid lifestyle choice for you, you might want to skip to the next barrier.

I have written about not putting any ideals or philosophies above the real children that you have in front of you. Now let's expand that to include not putting them above your very real spouse—and that includes things you read in this book.

Too many people sacrifice relationships after finding information in the world that speaks like a truth to them. I believe—and my research shows me—that the ideas in this book have led to healthier people and lives. I hope you think so too, but please do not use this book as a blunt force instrument. If someone you care about isn't there yet, don't hit them over the head with it.

Does the idea that it is important to support your child's interest resonate with your partner-in-parenting? If not, here are a few ways to think about this situation.

First, put them on a spectrum. What kind of a parent are they? Do they neglect, hurt, or harm your child? If they do, please put this book down and seek support and a safety plan.

If they do not, then what do they do? Do they provide shelter, money, food, help, time, love, humor, dishwashing, clothes mending, bread baking, candlestick making? If you've read anything on the five love languages (quality time, acts of service, physical touch, words of affection, gift-giving), they also work in family and parent dynamics. How and what does your partner provide?

This is, in short, a list of why you are grateful for them. Spend some time with it. Keep adding.

Exercise 13

What would you miss if they (your spouse) were gone?

What special skills do they have?

When you get home, what about the environment shows you that they are present?

How do your kids remind you of them?

I WANT to put you in a warm and fuzzy mood when thinking about your partner, so first, I am asking you to remember them at their best and think of them as being on the same team as you.

Remember that you are not always going to agree. Disagreement can happen over smaller things like TV show preferences and more important things like priorities in parenting. I often get clients who agree on so many things, but one parent is having difficulty getting behind their child's interest. Maybe they ignore it, or perhaps they actively encourage other activities that they value more. In turn, the other parent attempts to defend the child's interest, the time or cost involved, or even the child themselves. This resistance often leads to the first parent getting defensive, and it becomes an even bigger point of contention, creating a downward spiral.

Something else to consider is that this probably isn't about the actual interest. Often, Parent A sees Parent B's disapproval as indicative of something scarier, like a judgement of their abilities as a parent. Or, Parent A sees Parent B's objection as proof of an uglier truth about their spouse. For example, Parent B doesn't like their son to be in dance, and parent A immediately worries that they are sexist. Both parties are mad, scared, and sad, but if they can connect and talk on a more profound level—rather than continuing to argue on the surface level of the interest—progress can be made.

Realize that Parent B is allowed to have fears. Their fears might make you cringe, they might disappoint you, or they might seem baseless or silly, but they are their emotions and they are valid. Parents who have the most success working through these situations do so by breaking it down into two separate conversations: understanding and empathizing with their spouse's emotions, and then working through difficulties and finding solutions. I cannot emphasize this enough; these are two very different processes.

Sitting with another person's fears and feelings without trying to change them right away might be one of the greatest acts of love a person can give. When people feel like their worries are not being heard, they don't tend to feel like they can let them go and move on. If your partner is saying, "Hey, I have this concern," and you brush it off and essentially say, "Yeah, but you shouldn't," then they have no reason to believe that you are thoughtfully considering their perspective. Instead, show them that you take their feelings seriously.

They will no longer need to dig in their heels, tightening their grip on their fears.

Finally, be mindful of the fact that they are your child's other parent. If you were the first person in your partnership to pick up this book and read it, then chances are you are also the first one to read other parenting books and articles. You are probably also in parenting groups online, arranging the bulk of the play dates, making most of the activity schedules, and doing the volunteering. We tend to split the labor in families, so if you are reading this, I suspect you are carrying the managerial and emotional labor of your family. It can be really exhausting after all that work for someone else to come in and undermine or doubt your reasoning or research. Try to see this as one way they are asking to be involved. They are a parent too and on some level, they had a picture in their mind of what their family would look like and how their kids would be. They might even have childhood interests they hoped to pass along. It might be hard for them if their kids are not meeting those expectations, and it likely won't help to dismiss that and say they shouldn't be feeling those things. They are feeling them, and feelings are information. Is this a clue that they feel like they are missing out? Maybe there are ways to address that root feeling rather than making it about the child's specific interest area. Is this their way of wanting to connect, but they are unsure how they might get involved? Maybe they are not aware of anything beyond the stereotypes of that activity.

Most of these "maybes" have nothing to do with the kid. If you are so inclined, it would be an incredible act of love for everyone involved to help facilitate these deeper, more meaningful conversations, rather than staying on the surface, discussing whether or not they approve of a particular activity or interest.

BARRIER 12: IT IS ANNOYING

T hings really do become less annoying if you can look at them through your child's eyes. Watch those beautiful eyes light up. Look for the subtle changes in their face. Actively engage your curiosity about why they are so interested, rather than feeling annoyed. Be playful about finding the good in it, or the reasons why they enjoy it. That feels much more expansive than the tight, restrictive feeling of, "Oh no, they've turned to *that thing* again." Even that thought puts you on different teams. Finding the good is a muscle you can exercise.

Exercise 14

What is your kids most "annoying" interest?

Spend a short time describing why.

Okay, that's enough. You don't need to put any more energy into convincing yourself or anyone else how annoying it is. I believe you. I also know you can engage in consciously replacing those types of

Connect with Courage 137

thoughts with ones that encourage connection and a better relationship.

Why do you think your child likes this particular thing?

What good do you see in it? Write at least five positives about this interest.

Push yourself to add another one.

Are there any logistics you could change to minimize your annoyance? Can you wear headphones, for example? Try thinking first of things you can change, rather than asking that of your child.

BARRIER 13: I DON'T UNDERSTAND WHY THEY ENJOY IT

Some of the barriers to supporting our kids and their interests are logistical. It's about finding mentors or having enough space in your house for 80 trillion pieces of Lego. Others will be more internal and require self-reflection and honesty on your part. It might require a willingness to grow and change and allow your thoughts to shift. This barrier is one of those.

So, what if it's a topic or thing you don't love? What if you hate all things gory and they are super interested in horror movies?

Be curious about *why* it fascinates them.

It's like when your best friend has a super good friend—it's better for your relationship when you trust their opinion. I bet they collect good people you'd like, and if you get to know them, your life will expand and be richer for it. Your kid has an interest and I would bet you like your kid. Be open to expanding and enriching your own life.

I can imagine some of you protesting. More than just not liking your child's interest, you are afraid they are interested in something that is downright damaging (perhaps something violent). Or something that goes against your deeply held beliefs (you're vegan and your kid wants to spend their time smoking meats, for example).

Remember that **you** have a lifetime of experience and formed beliefs relating to how you feel about that thing. Your kid does *not* have the same relationship with it and therefore won't see it the same way. Allow it to mean something else to them. Get help processing your anxieties and fears. Part of their job in this life is to figure out who they are and what they believe, separate from you, their parent. If you choose to dig your heels in, it becomes about the power struggle rather than the stage of development they are going through. Instead, support them, be interested in their interests, and help them pursue these passions. Then one day if they start to question it, you will still have a relationship where they feel safe coming to you with their concerns and asking your opinion.

Exercise 15a

When you were growing up, was there a person that you *wished* showed more engagement in your interests?

I'm sorry they didn't show you more support. It's time to do some repairing, which may or may not involve them directly. I suggest that you seek therapy to work through this.

Do you know why they couldn't or didn't give you that support? Are they still around and influencing you? Write the answers to those questions.

IF YOU DON'T UNDERSTAND why your children enjoy something, it is your responsibility to do the work to change your negative thought process and your viewpoint, it is not their responsibility to change their interests or passion to accommodate you or make you more comfortable.

I have heard so many parents say that they don't understand why their kid "has to like *that thing*" because "it's gross, icky, mean, weird, violent, gory, silly, pointless, useless." Do any of those sound familiar?

Saying you don't understand why they enjoy something is admitting that you have not made the effort to better understand your child and their interest or to look at it from their perspective.

Finding yourself in this situation is a beautiful opportunity for connection between you and your kids. I want to use the example of YouTube toy-opening videos; I hear about those a lot. Have you seen them? Adults film themselves and/or their children opening wrapped toys. Sometimes the toys are small and hidden inside of eggs or encased in Play-Doh. Sometimes they hide them in backyards or playgrounds, and there is a hunting element to it. Sometimes it is just a video of an adults' hands as they open a toy package, describe what the toy is, and move on to the next one. Children are eating this up. I have heard from so many parents that they do not understand *why* their kid is so fascinated. The kid watching doesn't get to play with the toy. For the most part, the people on the videos aren't playing with them either—they really are just unwrapping them.

Take a minute to practice these new skills. What do you think a kid gets out of watching someone else open a toy? What feelings might it evoke? What processing happens in their brain? Do these videos remind you of something else?

Once I started paying attention, I noticed a few things. There are feelings of anticipation, and the thrill of getting clues, guessing, and using deductive reasoning. There is familiarity and comfort when the toys turn out to be a well-known franchise character. There is a certain element of slow-down-and-be-present and a restfulness. There is excitement without threat, danger, fear, or risk. It always turns out well. As for not opening the toy themselves, how many adults watch cooking shows without being able to taste the food themselves? Humans enjoy understanding other humans. We like to live vicariously; it connects us and helps us make sense of things. Toy unwrapping videos are a way to do that.

When you look at it that way, it begins to make a lot more sense, doesn't it?

Sometimes parents do not understand why their child likes to do the same thing over and over again. As I write this, I am sitting here with a television show on in the background that I have seen probably sixteen times. I know the story well and I know the music by heart. I know what is going to happen. Why do I go back to the same show?

Well, in one way it is practical. I don't need to focus on it. It's comforting background noise (and it has musical numbers, so bonus) but my thoughts can wander as I focus on what I am writing. Also, despite my many viewings, I often catch things that I did not notice before. With each new viewing, I can watch with a different focus. The first few times, it is usually about going along for the cinematic ride—your attention follows the carefully orchestrated decisions of the production and editing team. With subsequent viewings, you have more ability to look around. You can notice musical themes, storytelling devices, costume choices, camera angles. And if all of that wasn't enough, remember that saying about how you can never step in the same river twice? It isn't just the river that is changing. You aren't the same person doing the river-stepping, either. Have you ever had the experience of watching a show as a child, and then going back to watch it as an adult? It's a completely different thing! That's true even without years in between. Time and experience mean you view the same material differently.

Tradition is another possible reason for repeated viewings. I have known two separate individuals in my life who watched Dirty Dancing every day after school for approximately five years. It was a grounding and comforting tradition that provided them security.

Many of my clients, especially my self-aware teens and children, come to my office with increased anxiety. They are conscious of the large-scale problems and issues over which they have so little control. Watching the same show or playing the same game can be a way to have control over chaos.

It can also be atmosphere-setting. For example, I always listen to Hamilton when I need to get in the mood to do some serious deep cleaning.

I know their choice of how to spend their time can sometimes feel like it threatens your golden, glowing picture of what parenting and family are supposed to look like. When you don't personally understand the appeal of their interest, it is even harder, but here is your kid, giving you the key to a door into their world. They are telling you that they are interested in this thing or showing you through how they choose to spend their time. So, use it! Connect with it! Show a genuine interest in why they are interested in it!

Be interested in what your kid is interested in. Show active, engaged, and intelligent curiosity.

Exercise 15b

What is a question you have about their interest?

What are three questions and three follow up questions you can ask them?

What three places can you learn more about their interest?

What are three surprising facts you have learned?

Did it remind you of other things you might want to show your kid sometime?

Did it make you think of any potential gifts you could get your kid?

Can you think of any other person you might want to connect your kid with who shares their interest?

Can you think of any other resources you might want to connect your kid with? Groups, online or in-person?

Can you think of any places you might want to visit that are connected to your child's interest? Dream big! Brainstorm, don't edit here!

What are some other ways you can delve into your child's passion?

MANY OF US were ridiculed and shamed for our interests and passions growing up. It happens so often and so pervasively that it feels normal. It might be commonplace, but it isn't healthy. It's your job to recognize this and take active steps to remove it from your relationships.

"Love Poem," by John Frederick Nims, is read in many creative writing classes. Although the specifics of the woman he describes are not traditionally flattering, the poem is a great demonstration of how love is in the details.

> My clumsiest dear, whose hands shipwreck vases,
> At whose quick touch all glasses chip and ring,
> Whose palms are bulls in china, burs in linen,
> And have no cunning with any soft thing
>
> Except all ill-at-ease fidgeting people:
> The refugee uncertain at the door
> You make at home; deftly you steady
> The drunk clambering on his undulant floor.
>
> Unpredictable dear, the taxi drivers' terror,
> Shrinking from far headlights pale as a dime
> Yet leaping before apoplectic streetcars—
> Misfit in any space. And never on time.
>
> A wrench in clocks and the solar system. Only
> With words and people and love you move at ease;
> In traffic of wit expertly maneuver

And keep us, all devotion, at your knees.

Forgetting your coffee spreading on our flannel,
Your lipstick grinning on our coat,
So gaily in love's unbreakable heaven
Our souls on glory of spilt bourbon float.

Be with me, darling, early and late. Smash glasses—
I will study wry music for your sake.
For should your hands drop white and empty
All the toys of the world would break.

Learn the details. Show your child your love.

Exercise 15c

Who was most interested in your interests when you were younger?

How did it feel to have someone interested in your pursuits?

What did they do to show or tell you that?

BARRIER 14: FEAR OF JUDGMENT FROM OTHERS

Many people I work with want to parent differently because they want to break a family cycle, or because they do not want to parent in the same way as their parents. Lots of us have negative messaging—or dare I say it, baggage —that we carry from our childhoods into parenthood. Sometimes we are aware of it, can work through and process it, and prevent further damage from happening. Sometimes we can pinpoint the exact person whose judgmental voice is filling our head. Sometimes we can do this because that voice isn't in the past—they are in the here and now, making their opinion very known.

In my experience, we can sort them into three major categories: people we love and who love us; people who are invested in us but not always in a healthy way; and total strangers.

If the person judging your kid, or you, for their interest is a person you know loves you, why not start there? Remember that loving foundation you share, where questions might really be questions. If you are feeling judged, it might be your own insecurities surfacing. If you think there is something wrong with your child being deeply involved with their interest, it is much easier to assume that other people are also skeptical and to hear their innocuous comments as something more sinister.

If your child's interest is somewhat unconventional, and this person-you-know-loves-them is asking questions about more conventional things, remember that a lot of adults don't have great imaginations. They might be looking for a way to connect with your kid. If you assume the best of this person, you can help them connect.

For example, I know many families whose children are very interested in video games. If a grandparent were to ask them about what happened at school, or about what books they're reading, you could choose to look at that as a judgement on you for letting your children play video games. You could take it as an underhanded way of saying, "Your kids ought to be focused more on academics!" Or, you could remember that these adults love your kids and are grasping at straws, looking for a way to talk to them. You could, with confidence and peace of mind, reply, "Oh my gosh, they've been reading, and they have been so excited about this new game!" Step in and give them a bit of a prompt. Help them with that connection. They might just not have the knowledge or language to speak about your kids' interests. You might help them out at other times too, by sending photos along with helpful captions.

Even if these people-you-know-love-your-kid articulate their judgement a little more clearly and it is hard to give them the benefit of the doubt, it is helpful to remember that when you love someone, you often fear for them. When you fear for someone, it can often exert itself in the form of control.

As a parent, you can help run interference for your kids in a few ways. You can, without children present, remind those adults that this is a special occasion and you want to make sure they have fun. "No serious talk!" you might say, lightly, to lift any pressure they might be tempted to put on your kids. You might give a straightforward request not to speak about certain topics. You might prepare your kids ahead of time for questions those adults might ask and help them with a pat sentence or two they can respond with that will smooth the situation over. You can also remind those adults that they love your children, and that you want to make sure nothing gets in the way of their relationship. Invite them to see your children's successes in their interest, translate the lingo or jargon of the field, and celebrate their efforts with words like, "expert level," "mastery," "progressing," and "development."

This, however, is hard to do if you aren't feeling that way yourself. If you have secret, nagging fears about the validity of your children's interests, when a doubting voice enters your sphere, it is so easy to seize it and be seized by it. Don't let people who don't know your children as well as you do undermine your trust in them.

Looking at the second category, people vocalizing their doubts might not be coming from a real place of love. As the parent, that's your work to figure out. Are they a healthy person to include in your life? Do boundaries need to be established or upheld? Do you need to think creatively about the logistics of seeing each other to minimize this type of judgement? For some families, it is as simple as making sure they go to a movie or go bowling when they see each other so that there is something else to focus on, rather than sitting down at a restaurant where more critical talk might happen.

It is important to remember that the criticisms these folks level at you say more about them than they do about your kid. We recognize faults in others that align with our own insecurities.

Do what you can to protect your children from verbal onslaughts of criticism given under the guise of love.

As for the third category, if these people are random strangers in restaurants or grocery stores, it is time to do some self-reflective work on why those opinions matter so much to you. It's not about the checker at the store who quizzed your kid's spelling and raised their eyebrows when they responded with rapid-fire Minecraft dialogue. It's about you and your own fears. Check that. Do enough personal work so that when a random stranger tells your Pokémon-Go-wielding kid that, "Screen time will rot your brain," you can confidently dismiss this statement and replace it with reality. Not for the stranger's benefit but for your kid, who is watching and absorbing. Do your research. Trust your children. Go to bat for them.

BARRIER 15: I DON'T THINK THEY'LL BE SUCCESSFUL OR MAKE MONEY

L et's talk about the definition of success. What is it? You could make two lists right now —the definition of success as your culture/society sets it, and your definition of success for your children. Is there any overlap?

When asked, many well-meaning parents say something like, "I want my children to have a good job, a good relationship, enough money, and to be happy."

Some parents skip saying all of that, and say they want, "Success and a good education," for their children. Or, "A high paying job." But when pressed, it usually comes down to them wanting elements in their children's lives that help them feel fulfilled and happy, however that might look.

The pretty well-accepted version of success I have gathered involves some of the following:

- Money (enough to eat what you want, travel, live where you want)
- Relationships (romantic and otherwise)
- Exposure (to academic subjects, to diverse ideas and lifestyles)

- Fulfillment (with job or career, or choice not to have one, creative outlets)
- Choice (of career, of kids, of number of houseplants)

Take each one of those elements of success and play it out. Make a list of what that looks like for you, and what that would look like for your child. Again, those are two different lists. You are not your child. Your child is not you. The tools, traits, skills, and lessons you needed to learn to have success are not necessarily the same ones your children need. In fact, I could make a pretty safe bet that they are definitely *not* the same. Your kids are growing up in a different historical, societal, technological, and cultural context than you did. Success will be measured differently. Help them discover how they learn, how to work others, think divergently, solve problems, and trust themselves. Those are powerful traits for explorers setting off into the unknown. In some ways, they are better equipped than you are to figure out the other things they need to be successful for their time and place. Help them make connections and value themselves by encouraging their interests and protecting their passions.

One relatively simple way to help facilitate interests and practice supporting them is by bringing your kid food while they game, watch, play, craft, etc.

Exercise 16a

What is your child's favorite food?

What are five other foods they also like?

What are three snacks that you can bring that won't make sticky fingers (not great for game playing)?

What are you worried will happen if you bring them food or otherwise facilitate their activity?

OFTEN, parents are afraid that their kids are never going to grow up and do _____ for themselves. They worry that helping kids now will mean they will not be self-sufficient or successful later. I want to suggest the somewhat radical idea that you don't get to be in control of exactly what your kids are learning from any given situation.

You might think that by making them eat meals at the table you are teaching them to value their family. Instead, they may well be getting the impression that their opinions don't matter. Or maybe you believe that by requiring them to prepare their own snacks they will learn self-sufficiency and that bringing them food might teach them dependency. It's more likely to show them how to be thoughtful, caring, nurturing, generous, and giving, demonstrating that you support and value their choices, and by extension, support and value *them.*

Exercise 16b

What are some other things you might be saying with a loving and generous offering of food?

Perhaps you are communicating things like, "I am thinking about you," "I like to be nurturing," "I know that you like this," "I want to help you keep doing what you love and choose to do without needing to stop."

You might think it odd that I went from a big picture conversation about success to "Slice up some apples." This was purposeful. When you find yourself drifting too far into the abstract future, get back to your real, present kid. This is always a good practice.

There are so many ways to communicate love to your kids!

Another is to generously give your time or service.

What are three ways you can *show* your love without disrupting what they've chosen to do right now?

Take this opportunity and do one of them.

BARRIER 16: IT'S MESSY

Subtitle: It's not really about the mess. (Sometimes it's about the mess.)

There are two things I want to talk about in this section. First, the benefits of mess, and second, ways to make things less messy.

Yes. Often our kids' interests are messy in their own right. I only need to say the word "Lego" for a deep, visceral reaction from most parents. Sometimes the interest itself relies on lots of supplies or many parts and it naturally creates a mess. Other times any one thing might not be a huge disaster, but your child jumps from activity to activity, leaving pile after pile in their wake. Your kid might be the type who makes a mess of a project and then wails if you try to straighten it up, worried you'll disturb something. They also tend to be the type of kid who doesn't want a single thing moved because they are "in the middle of it." And they could be "in the middle of it" for weeks!

So, what are some possible reasons for a mess?

The first thing is that the creative part of our brain works better when it's *not* working alongside the editing part. There's a section on brainstorming ideas in this book—the same concept applies when it's physical toy parts and art supplies. Creativity happens when you let it go unchecked.

When I was 14 or so, I was very into making zines. I would spend hours (sometimes upward of 14 to 16 hours at a time) on my bedroom floor cutting and rubber-cementing tiny pieces of paper and poetry to each other. If you looked down at me from above, it would look like a tornado, with me and my scissors in the eye of the storm. It was important to me to do it all in one sitting; even listening to the same album over and over again. That way the whole zine felt cohesive, evoking a harmonious atmosphere. A friend of mine once described me as, "Trying to take a sip from a firehose." Looking back, that's exactly how it felt. I had outpourings of creativity. I needed all of the outlets. I needed all the things at my fingertips because everything could be connected, and I was making those connections.

If my mother or father had come in at hour two and said, "You've been doing this long enough and it is too messy. Time to clean up," it would have felt like legitimate torture. It would have put a pause— and maybe a permanent halt—on the creative process. Often, I would collage with something that I had cut off of something else. At the earlier time I thought it was trash, but then found a use for it. If I had been made to straighten up periodically, I would not have had those bouts of inspiration, creativity, and resourcefulness.

So, there are benefits to mess. There are benefits to clutter; you can see connections, putting things together in ways that were not originally intended. These are excellent qualities to foster in children. We want children to be creative thinkers, problem solvers, and innovators. It benefits our kids and the entire world if they can look at a problem in front of them and come up with outside-of-the-box solutions. To get there, they need the adults in their lives to let them dump everything out of the boxes and make those connections.

At some point in my life, I realized that although I wanted everything at my fingertips during the creative process, I worked even better if I started with a clean slate. I liked having materials organized so that I could find them quickly when I needed them. I learned that if I started with a trash can near me, I could put scraps in there along the way if I wanted to. I figured out that at certain times in my collaging and art-making I liked to do a little clearing up, so that I could have a bit of a mid-session fresh start. I learned that I enjoyed a combination of organization and clutter—and that different times called for different levels. No one else could come into my process and know when I was ready for a shift. If someone else came in and cleaned up while I was working, it would cause tightness and stress and panic. It would be a barrier to creativity and to our relationship.

I do like things organized. I see the value and benefit of a clear workspace and easy to find supplies. I know that when multiple people are living in a house, it can even be dangerous or painful to leave full-blown creative messes out at all times. I've compiled a list of possible solutions. A starting place for you to think creatively about how to respect your mess maker's process while making it a functional living space.

I want to highly discourage making specific rules such as, "You must clean everything up before dinner," or "You are only allowed to get two tubs out at a time." Rules that you set ahead of time are arbitrary. They do not take into account the reality of your child's wants or interests or situational changes.

Instead of rules, try shifting some of the logistics so that it's more manageable. Be sure to pay attention to any voice that says, "You have to." Where is that coming from? It's not about your child.

Pare down where possible

Don't get rid of other people's things—that's not nice—but you can cut back on different types of clutter. For example, I didn't want to cast out toys, so I cut down on the sheer number of dishes my household has. Every dish can be dirty, and it's still just about one dishwasher load worth. That cuts down on the overall sense of clutter in a house without curtailing the kids' interests.

Look for ways to do less cleaning

Try using disposable paper goods for a week or two, or during particularly busy times. I am a professor and two times a semester, I have no time for anything else. While I'm grading midterms and finals, the last thing I want to see are dishes piling up. I pull out the paper plates for those weeks, and everyone is happier.

Think about the timing

There are times when I just want to be able to walk through my doors to a house that doesn't look like a disaster. Can the kids go outside for a little while? Or even get into the car while you run around and straighten up before leaving the house? Leave, go to a park, the library, a movie, whatever, then you get to have the experience of walking through the door again to a (relatively speaking) clean house.

Use other spaces

You can support your child's ceramic interest without turning your living room into a clay pit. There are studios, parks, maker spaces, libraries, recreation centers, and friends.

Get help

There are many kids or teens out there who would like to earn money, either by helping put away or organize supplies or by hanging out with your kids while you do it. Barter. Think creatively. When my children were small and nursing, it was easier to do social media work than clean the house. I found a very limited-time opportunity doing social media for a restaurant, in exchange for exactly the amount of money I needed for a semi-regular housekeeper.

Make it faster to clean up when you do

Put everything in tubs! Everything. Seriously. Tubs. If it's for large items, make them big, clear, stackable with locking lids. Put photos of the type of thing that goes in them, if you want non-reading kids to be able to toss things in the right place. If you have too many things for a tub, then go one-category more specific. For example, I have too many "office supplies" so I split "scissors and glue" from "pens and pencils." If I had too many pens and pencils, I'd split again.

When you are putting things in tubs, think realistically about how you will use them. For some people, it might make sense to have all the paint in one tub and all the paintbrushes in another. However, I find that it's more effective to put everything you need for a single project in a tub. I have a combination: some tubs are just yarn, some are just crochet hooks. But when I'm in the middle of a project, there is a tub that has all the yarn, crochet hooks, and instructions that I need for that whole project. That means when it's time to clean up, it all goes into the same tub—I don't have to work on splitting it between three or four tubs. It makes cleaning much faster.

Start projects on tarps or a big blanket—something easy to lift the corners, shake everything to the middle, and then sort and dump in a tub. Or, use one of those big grocery-store mops to shove everything into the middle!

Do messy stuff in the kitchen or bathroom where it's easier to wipe down or spray down. Invest in a kiddie pool or two for the living room.

Use baby gates or other creative ways to set stuff up—barriers in the house to slow the spread. Mostly you won't need to say, "Don't take this past this point." Think of it as resource management; the way land managers direct crowds in a National Park. People and things usually take the path of least resistance, even without someone with a megaphone standing around and giving them directions.

Think big impact

Does it make a big visual difference in your world to have the dining room table cleared? Just do that.

Don't get too precious about your furniture

Especially when kids are little. There is some element of destruction and creativity and kids that all go together. Maybe instead of a new couch, prolong its life so that you don't worry so much about keeping things "nice." Get a slipcover for when company comes and think of the old couch as an investment in your mental health.

Keep a private space

Instead of feeling like you have to have your whole living space perfect, maybe create a small and sacred retreat for yourself.

Close doors

Set up messy stuff in places that have doors to close on them. We have culturally imposed ideas of the uses of rooms in houses. What if you put a dining room table in the bedroom, because that's where they mostly want to paint, and that way you can just close the door when it's messy? What if you put wood vinyl flooring in a bedroom, even though usually they have carpet, because it makes it easier to clean? Of course, each family's resources are part of the conversation, but the creative thinking behind it is all the same. Think outside the norm to discover solutions that work for your family.

You don't have to provide access to everything all at once

Once you have everything in tubs, it's easier to rotate through them anyway. Put half of them somewhere harder to get to and every few months pull out different ones. It's like shopping in your own closet.

Absence can make the heart grow fonder, and it's fun to rediscover long lost loves.

Maybe you know your kid often jumps to new things that aren't connected and it would make everyone happier to put away one thing before getting the next thing out. Do it for them, if you can. That's sweet. Or cheerfully suggest that they put away the Play-Doh before getting out the puzzles.

Make a game out of cleaning

Depending on your kids' developmental stage, they might enjoy a racing game: "I'll time you to see how fast you can put five things away and then time you again to see if you beat it!" Or a categorizing game: "Let's put all of the yellow things in here!" Or a game of "Simon Says," or an accuracy-throwing-game, or a sing-song game. Get creative.

Sometimes it's about your attitude

Do you grumble while you put away stuffed animals for the nine-hundred-millionth time? Or do you sing while you and little cartoon birdies work? If you're somewhere in between, be conscious of the message about straightening up that you're sending. Say things out loud like, "I enjoy clearing this table." "It feels so good to start a new project with all this space!" "I love to make a space feel beautiful and peaceful!" "It makes me so happy to put away all these toys because I know how much you love playing with them all at once."

That one goes back to the *why* you're cleaning at all. Are you cleaning because you think you're supposed to? Because there is some internal voice that feels like it's making you? Check that at the door. Really. Are you cleaning because you really believe and have watched your kids and know that everyone functions better with a clear and open space? That's a wonderful gift you can give them, so act like it. Be nurturing, if that's why you're doing it. No one wants a gift if the gift-giver is grumbling while they give it.

Think realistically about the "have to" feelings. What would honestly happen if you didn't clean that thing? Not, "It would be a mess." Yes, but what *happens* if it's a mess? Seriously? Examine your thinking.

Engage more

There is something that happens to parents when they stand aside, watching while their kids make a mess. Resentment builds. Burnout flares. If you're right there in the middle of it, though, it changes your perspective. Lie on your stomach in the middle of that mess and see it from their point of view. See how it's not a pile of trash, but a magical kingdom full of possibilities. Watch their eyes light up as they explain it to you. Try to see it how they see it. Try really, really, *really* hard.

I could write another whole book about parental roles, emotional labor, and household/parenting management. If you are choosing to support your children's interest and one of the barriers for you is messiness, then this applies. And I want you to always be thinking of it as a choice. If you are feeling burned out *and* it is your choice to do this, pay attention to those burned-out feelings. It can be so exhausting to feel isolated in your house with kids and cleaning to do. In my case, I am an extreme extrovert. Too many days at home is draining (two days is my limit). I try to pay attention to that and have people over who know I'll be puttering or putting away laundry or crocheting while they are over.

I make sure I have time for my projects, but my quantity had to adjust with children. I remember I invited these kids into the world, they are my guests. When I invite someone over, I sometimes have to adjust my expectations to be a good host. I do not get to spend four hours a day crocheting. I just don't. However, I crochet nearly every day, even if it's for only a few minutes. I think of it as concentrated crochet time. It is a myth that you need hours and hours away from your children for "me time" to refresh yourself. What is truly impactful is the intent behind the time. The other little-spoken-secret is that the more you lean into engaging with your kids, the more your feelings of burnout and exhaustion decrease. You don't see the mess as something to resent that takes time away from what you want. You see the mess as beautiful evidence of love and childhood, and something you helped to protect. That is refreshing. That is the antidote to burnout.

This will all change, very, very quickly. Whatever phase of life you and your children are in will change faster than you know. Do you remember when it seemed like all of life was diapers and strollers and drooling and teething? That's gone now. This will be too. Sometimes that thought can be a positive one—to remember that challenging things will shift. Sometimes it's a tragic thought—to remember that beautiful moments will change. Let that be a catalyst for enjoying your children right now, as they are, mess and all. Let that be a catalyst to jump in and join in. Set aside the voice that says something "has to be a certain way" and do what works for your family. Do not waste more time in resentment or frustration.

Be grateful for that mess

Be grateful for those kids. Be grateful that you have the resources that become clutter. Be grateful that you have the space that is being cluttered. Be grateful you have this time with those children. Use reframing techniques. When you look at a mess and heave a deep sigh and see the time it will take to clean it, actively turn that sigh into a deep breath and think to yourself, "I am so lucky to have these children." Because you are.

My son wanted some curio shelves for all his tiny treasures. I found some for $6 each, out of lightweight unfinished craft wood. They have a plexiglass cover that slides on. We painted them together (he loves turquoise!) and now he is happy to have his things safe, dust-Free, and out of the way!

I find it really satisfying in general when I can find ways to help him organize and enjoy his things. He likes to collect this and that and it's fun to see his pride in displaying his stuff.

When he was littler, he loved rocks and fossils and I found a great place that had cheap wooden boxes (similar to the wood in these shelves) with clear tops, so he could create a kind of geological/archaeological museum on his dresser. Craft shops are good resources for little paintable storage solutions made out of wood and paper mache."

— SHANNON

BARRIER 17: I THINK SCREEN TIME IS BAD

Why is playing video games one of the absolute best things a kid can do for their well-being, especially if undergoing trauma, abuse, or even "just" a difficult time? Here are seven reasons why:

1. We deal even when we don't talk. Our brains are processing. We don't always need to do it out loud. Have you ever been troubled about something and gone to bed, then had a solution when you woke up? Video games can provide that type of time.

2. For kids especially, having a sense of power when they have gone through abuse or trauma or are feeling overwhelmed and out of control is super important. Video games and play are excellent ways for kids to get a sense of empowerment and mastery To feel like, "I've got this." They literally have the controls in their hands. I cannot stress enough how important this is.

3. We cannot talk about heavy topics all the time. Our brains need a break. Use video games as a distraction and see that as a good thing!

4. Studies have shown that after trauma, video game playing is one of the best ways to minimize potential PTSD symptoms, particularly flashbacks and unwanted sudden recall. It does not diminish a person's ability to recall information or details when they want, but increased gameplay helps with unwanted memories. This finding is huge for the field of trauma work, and great news for parents who struggle to help their kids when they go through hard times.

5. Gameplay of all types can be a foundation for healthier relationships, especially if the players don't have good attachment or they have a reason to distrust. Accomplishing goals together, seeking out resources together ... such a valuable tool for the adults as well. I play games in therapy sessions to build rapport. It works. There's science about why, but anyone who has ever played a game with anyone else knows this!

6. Video games provide tools for social, emotional, mental, and physical resilience. You gain optimism, seek out allies, use resources. Again, this is so important for all kids, and especially children who have been through trauma.

7. When you value their interests, you are showing them you trust and respect them. When kids are abused or mistreated, it shakes the foundation of their identity and it is even more vital for them to learn how to trust themselves. A relatively easy way to do that is for us to trust how they spend their time. Let them play. I can't think of a better tool for kids who have been through abuse or are going through difficulties than playing lots of video games with the trustworthy adults in their life.

I want to address "screen time" specifically. Technology can change so fast. Many of my favorite parenting books have no mention of YouTube, because there was no YouTube when they were written. I am probably dating this book just by putting it in here, because who knows what medium we will be using in 3, 5, or 15 years, but I think that it's important to talk about now. If everything changes and people in the future read this and roll their eyes at the reference, well, future-parents, I don't know what you'll need, but I do know that the principles will be the same. Take what I'm saying here about YouTube and generalize it to whatever the current-thing-your-children-are-super-into-but-you-don't-totally-understand is.

First, I want to talk about the phrase, "screen time." It's dismissive. It really is. Don't get defensive. Yes, I know what you mean when you say it, but you're lumping many, many things together in a way that effectively says, "I know you have this interest because you spend a lot of time doing it but I am not going to be bothered to learn the details." It's like when someone watches me crochet and calls it, "sewing." I can forgive the ignorance of strangers. When a family member does it, it's a little bit heartbreaking. I want them to know me well enough to know that when I'm using one hook, I'm crocheting. And that I'm probably crocheting because it's the thing I've done longer and I'm more comfortable with. I do enjoy knitting, but I usually knit when I am working on a specific project for someone, but when I'm making up my own pattern, I am crocheting. We all want to be known. Using specific language when referring to a person's interest is one way to show that we know them.

This is an important task. If you honestly don't know what it is your kids are using those screens for, take the time to learn. Watch and pay attention.

Exercise 17

First, which types of screens do they seem to prefer, and at what times? Maybe they are on consoles in the morning, laptops in the afternoon, the big screen TV after dinner, and on a tablet at night.

Why do you think that is? Are there physical or logistical reasons? Maybe certain people only play certain games with them at certain times because of the time differences between your locations. Maybe their favorite YouTuber releases new videos at certain times of day. Maybe they enjoy taking a bit of a mental break at a certain point in the day, so they want to lay down and relax, and a handheld device is more conducive to that. There is a reason. Care enough to figure it out. They might not even be conscious of it, but you can be.

Once you've pinpointed the types of screens, here's the next fun detective part. What *exactly* are they doing on them? Just off the top of my head, are they... Playing a game? Is it a battle, first-person shooter, world-building, crafting, map-based? Are they selling on Etsy? Posting on Deviantart? Looking at art? Getting ideas for food, workouts, or cosplay on Pinterest? Are they watching YouTube? Exploring tutorials, famous people, or musicians? Are they watching clips of the news or comedians? Are they talking to friends? Faceting family? Reading books or fan fiction? Posting self-esteem-boosting selfies? Are they researching? Forming social connections? Looking up favorite actors on IMDb? Updating their water intake on *Plant Nanny?* Checking off goals or tasks?

What are they doing? Be specific.

HERE's a list of the things I have personally done on devices with screens in the last 24 hours: Scheduled clients, updated my Patreon page, written in a journal, made a grocery list, listened to *The Railway Children*, updated my *Plant Nanny* app, used my *SuperBetter* app, talked to my husband, my mother, my sisters, and my three best friends, photographed my kids, worked on a bio for a conference, did marketing for my private practice, posted on social media for a few businesses, saw a client, looked up resources for a client, played *Settlers of Catan*, played *2048*, took a selfie, connected with an exercise group, looked at animal pictures, posted a few memes, saved crochet patterns on Pinterest, purchased yarn, ordered a few kitchen gadgets and work supplies on Amazon, looked up a recipe, looked up a restaurant on Yelp, ordered delivery, made a grocery list, researched medication for a sick family member, made a workout playlist, watched a workout video, used *Zombie Run* app, posted in running accountability group, read research about gratitude and goal-setting, managed finances, set up a spreadsheet for my husband, looked up exploding experiments for my kids, found the name of a Hatchimal, wrote this section of the book...

Those are the actions. Here are some of the real things that happened:

I connected with people by speaking on the phone, video chatting, "liking" their social media posts, cheering them on when they accomplished a run, posting memes and playing games with them. Social connection is important. Isolation is a significant factor in many mental health conditions, both as a root cause and as an exacerbating element. Connecting with other people is made vastly easier with the aid of screen-based devices.

I expressed myself creatively. I photographed, added filters, cut, cropped, and edited artwork.

I refreshed myself. I spent some time listening to books, playing games, giving my busy brain a few minutes to soak things in.

I made connections. I have long been a fan of Edward Eager, who pays many homages to *The Railway Children* books but had never read them. I looked up resources for a client and connected new treatment language with other therapeutic ideologies.

I learned about new treatment options for mental health conditions and about marketing.

I furthered my career.

I helped people.

I trusted myself and what I needed. I worked when I could, I took breaks when I deemed it best. I prioritized my time and my to-do list.

I nurtured my home and my family, both by doing some of these things with them like watching YouTube videos, by getting items we needed, and by focusing on the ordinary details of the day through photographing them.

Sometimes we are taken in by sensationalist news coverage. "Screens make our eyes melt!" "Television for kids under 5 transforms them into aliens!" "The dreaded tablet will come into your home and divide children from their parents and turn them into zombies!" Remember what sort of news sells: the kind that scares people. Make a peaceful parenting decision to stop watching or reading that sort of news coverage. When you are exposed to it, look at it critically. How long ago was the study done? Was it performed with a large enough sample size? How was it conducted? Who did the actual research, and who paid for it? What do they gain when parents are afraid?

A helpful way to alleviate your own fear is whenever you hear the voice inside saying, "Ahh! But screens! They're bad! Ahh!" substitute the word "book" for "screen." Pretend that they are sitting there with a book. Does your heart rate slow? Do you look at them with pride? Would you feel better if they were reading for hours every day? Why is that any different?

Part of why it's different is the cultural morality we impose on certain things; particularly new things and things that younger generations enjoy. Not valuing what young people use, like, or bring to the table is a form of ageism. Don't be a fuddy-duddy. You might not understand it, but that doesn't mean you have to be a classic tired trope and be fearful of it. Be curious instead. Be on their side.

BARRIER 18: I NEED ME TIME

There are times when you feel the pull of a thousand weighty expectations, the lure of other projects, and the siren call of what-your-friends-are-doing. You will see ads for spas and travel; activities for people with time who get to use it in a downright luxurious fashion. You will get resentful of building another Lego tower, of watching another minute of a Minecraft YouTube channel, and of cleaning up another sticky, paint-scattered mess. As a mother, as a therapist, and especially as a person who has a masterfully cultivated to-do list three miles long there is one big, big secret: nothing will make you feel better or more replenished than putting aside all the other things and playing with your kids. I mean it.

There are hundreds of self-help books, podcasts, videos, and groups out there telling you to take more time away from your kids to have more time for yourself. Carve out that time, no matter what—schedule it, put it on your calendar, make it sacred and precious. I think it is important to do things that interest you. Still, any time someone is recommending hard-and-fast distance from your kids as the cure for burnout I think, sadly that they have never felt the adrenaline-filled joy of an impromptu living room dance party with a bunch of kiddos. They have never felt the deep satisfaction of putting aside their phone, laying themselves on the floor to get a kids' eye view, and helping build that intricate tower or puzzle or mud pie. They have never thrown their hands over their head in triumphant victory, side by side with their kid on a game. Lean into it, not away from it.

When you take time away from your kids, it doesn't help with deep feeling; it's only a temporary breather. It's like taking a hit off an oxygen machine. It helps, but it doesn't actually repair your lungs. Full-hearted presence with your kids is the magic that heals what needs fixing inside.

While taking time away might make some of the noise or overwhelm go away and help you think clearly for a minute, in my experience it also adds an element of guilt, distance, barriers to connection, and resentment when going back to them. There is the presence of more complex emotions: shame, embarrassment, irritation, annoyance, desperation, sadness, restriction. These feelings are barriers to your relationship and to your well-being.

Maybe you feel that you lack resources. Diving into parenting can help heal you. It's called "restorative parenting," and it's a wonderful thing. It's like time travel. Like magic. It's like being able to go back and restore old hurts to full health. Have you ever noticed that when you do something differently or better than your parents did, you not only get a sense of satisfaction but also something deeper out of it? Being a better parent is not only good for your kids, it is good for you too. In the therapy world, we often talk about the sad or hurt child we used to be, and how we carry those little boys and girls around inside of us as adults. Diving into the joys and wonders and interests of your children is good for them and your relationships, and it is also healing for you.

Take a minute to think about the messages you've received about "me time." I am not suggesting that you never again pick up a paintbrush, a knitting needle, or go for a walk in nature alone. I am reminding you, however, that kids are not little forever and before you know it, you will have more time for yourself. I am asking you to remember that you invited your children here, and it is your privilege to make it the most wonderful and rich experience you can. I am asking you to choose them. I think many parents have the experience of being with their kids physically without being fully present with them. Those times tend to breed the most resentment due to being pulled in multiple directions. Next time, instead of reaching for a solo activity, experiment with replenishing yourself through their laughter, their curiosity, and the sound of their voice. Try putting down your phone and watching their YouTube video. Or saying, "Hey, I want to do some painting. Want to come and paint with me?" Be sure to notice the small and pleasurable details of their face and hands. To take a deep breath and inhale the absolute miracle that is the combination of events that had to happen to get you and that person on the planet at the same time, and exhale the over-stated falsehood that, to feel fulfilled, you need more time away from them.

Exercise 18

What are you hoping to get out of self-care? What do you feel like you are missing right now? What is empty that needs filling?

What are some activities you did before you had kids that you haven't done for a while?

Are you missing the activity? Is there a part of your identity that seems to have changed without that interest in your life?

How would you have described yourself in the past?

How do you describe yourself now?

What are some ways you could include your children in those activities?

What are some of your children's interests that seem the most fun to you, personally?

What are a few ways you can make sure to incorporate those into your next few days?

Write about the last few times you felt truly alert and focused on your kids without distraction. Include the setting, atmosphere, and how you felt before and after.

THERE IS a certain kind of gratitude that you can practice and exercise, like any muscle: be actively grateful that you have your children here with you. In my profession I work with many parents who are dealing with the grief of having lost a child. I want you to do a really hard thing for a minute. Imagine what would happen if they weren't here. It is such a terrible thought that most parents won't let it in. If it tries to creep closer, most of us shove it away. Take a minute and open up the gate behind which that fear is always lurking. Imagine your tomorrow if something were to happen to your child today. My throat clenches. My stomach aches. It is nearly unbearable to even contemplate. And yet, this is the reality that many parents have to live with, minute by excruciating minute. That throat-clenching-stomach-aching feeling is information. It is an expression of love. Many parents have lost children. Many people want to have children and can't. You get to have yours here. If you knew your time was limited, what would you do? Would you want more "me time" or would you hunker down next to them and ask about their favorite movies, music, or Pokémon? Your time with them *is* limited. Be grateful for the minutes you have and act accordingly. Practice gratitude often. We all know people who would give up anything for one more minute of play with their child. You are lucky to have your kid in front of you. Don't squander those amazing, limited, uncertain minutes.

Share your interests with your kids. Bring them into it. Be overjoyed, welcoming, and contagious with the pleasure of hosting. And when your kids say, as mine are right now, "Mama, come play puppets with us!" Put down your laptop and write another day.

I try very hard to support my children's interests, and my own experiences guided me. My eight year-old had read everything she could, watched everything she could, about Egyptian Death Rites. At a museum, she corrected the docent about information given, and was right! Fortunately, the docent respected my child's knowledge and encouraged her to use her voice. It was such a pleasure to watch other museum goers ask my child questions and have her answer them with confidence. These type of incidents, which happened regularly, helped with my fears. Seeing my children as adults, confident and sure of themselves, has been worth it.

— Joylyn

BARRIER 19: I WANT THEM TO HAVE BALANCE

In the mental health world, we discuss the concept of balance a lot. A lot, a lot. I have one pretty simple statement about this concept: balance is overrated.

Are you on a bike? Fine; talk about balance. Are you working on a budget? Okay, you're good to go. But if you're talking about the idea that we must maintain equilibrium and peacefulness in all things at all times—that is a false ideal state and aiming for that can come at the expense of other things.

As a society, we expend a tremendous amount of energy in trying to be balanced, even-keeled, or moderate. A sense of decorum and calm is considered virtuous. We have visions of early morning stretching routines and setting intentions and staying in a state of total gratitude all day, and if we fail to accomplish this, there is something wrong with *us*, not the premise.

Exercise 19

At a conference, I asked the audience what roles they or their partner expected them to be, in addition to their role as "parent." Before reading our brainstormed list, write your list. (Examples to get you started: chauffeur, housekeeper, scheduler...)

We brainstormed the following:

Accountant, advocate, archivist, art critic, back-up dancer, back-up singer, banker, caregiver, carpenter, chef, chauffeur, cheerleader, clown, coach, comedian, confidante, consultant, counselor, costume designer, cruise director, dictionary/thesaurus, DJ, doctor, dog walker, editor, educator, face painter, financial planner, form-filler, hair stylist, housekeeper, interpreter, jungle gym, landscaper, launderer, legal aid, librarian, life coach, nurse, nutritionist, masseuse, mediator, musician, party planner, photographer, project manager, promoter, proofreader, publicist, scheduler, referee, researcher, scapegoat, seamstress, shopper, social coordinator, sounding board, special event coordinator, stylist, teacher, tech support, therapist, translator, travel agent, wardrobe assistant, zookeeper.

When you stop and take a look at that list, it's overwhelming. We expect so much of ourselves and feel the need to do it all with poise, grace, and Zen. We strive for an ideal that is impossible to reach and then disparage ourselves for not reaching it.

That list gives us a strong sense of how much we try to take on as parents.

Now give yourself two columns. In the left column, write the 20 most frequently asked-of-you roles in. In the right column, write which domain you believe it mostly falls into: physical support, social support, mental support, logistical/functional support, or emotional support.

Which of the roles in this list do you really, truly love being for your family?

Which of these feels like the biggest struggle?

Which domains do the biggest struggles typically fall under for you? Is there a pattern?

Which roles in this list do you feel like you spend the majority of your time being?

Do you spend more time acting in roles you struggle with, or ones in which you feel you excel?

When there is an area in which we struggle, we feel that we should spend more time focused on improving that area. The result is we spend more time and energy doing something that feels difficult, brings stress or tension, has negative or shameful feelings associated with it, or leads to negative and berating self-talk. It also means we spend less time doing things that make us feel positive, competent, and good about ourselves. What could happen if we shift those proportions and use our superpowers instead?

What happens when we stay in a space of feeling not-good-enough for extended periods? We don't let ourselves excel. We don't feel competent. We don't experience mastery, success, or pride. We constantly feel like we aren't measuring up.

Is this what you are cultivating for your children too?

Because we expect this of ourselves, it often translates into what we expect of our kids. They are showing you their superpowers and it's your job to recognize them.

What are three of your parenting superpowers? Which of the above roles do you feel especially competent at?

What are three of your kids' superpowers?

How do they show you their superpowers?

THAT LIST UP THERE? Choose three and focus on those. You've got this. Forgive yourself for falling short on the rest—it's just too much. That's one of the negative impacts of falling for the idea that balance is key; we spread ourselves too thin trying to do it all.

It's one thing if we adults throw time, energy, and money at trying to be something we aren't while feeling guilty or ashamed that we can't reach that perceived state of perfection. But when we project that idea on our children, it can be harmful. It means we are holding up an imagined ideal of our child instead of paying attention and appreciating the actual person right in front of our eyes. If we are focused on balance, we lose track of the benefits of depth.

Stop thinking of balance through the lens of what happens within a 12 or 24-hour period. Don't even think about balance in terms of a week. If you must, think about a balanced month, or better yet, a balanced year. When you look back over your last year, do you see a sense of balance? If you were to make a graph of your children's interests, over the previous week they might be heavily weighted in one column. But if you were to expand the time frame to a year, chances are it levels out. Look at the big picture.

Following a passion deeply is not negative. Look at it as commitment, dedication, investment, and mastery. Those are resume-worthy words. Those are qualities that people in charge of admissions and hiring are looking for.

SECTION V

BRAINSTORMING

NOTES ON BRAINSTORMING

I think brainstorming is an incredibly important, often overlooked skill. To successfully brainstorm, you have to be able to put aside your inner (or outer) editor, be playful, and let all the ideas have free and wild rein. If your editor is present, some ideas will not feel free to come out. Even by yourself, your self-consciousness gets in the way of making potentially ridiculous suggestions that could lead to great ideas. Brainstorming can lead to a wonderful orchard full of fruit to choose from.

I was once in a room brainstorming how to get campers from the parking lot where their parents were dropping them off, to the camp up the mountain. I asked the group for ideas—with the caveat that, for fifteen minutes, no idea was too silly. People suggested busses, cars, and then got sillier: flying carpets, hot air balloons, and elephants. The idea of using elephants sparked an idea of using pack mules, which could tie into the historically themed portion of the camp. Suddenly, the whole program solidified in my mind, and I could see the mission statement of the camp and how other logistical decisions could support it. I made this connection because someone suggested using elephants! This suggestion made the overall theme and program of the camp that much richer and would not have been possible if I had started with criticism or told participants why their ideas wouldn't work as soon as they suggested them.

Criticism is death to brainstorming. It is an important skill, but it needs to happen at a separate time, in a different step of the decision-making process.

When we think of the things our children are interested in, we often come to the table with criticism already present.

This section is my solo-venture into brainstorming with you about your kid's interest. I want you to do something: take your hands and cup them close to your mouth, as though you are holding something small and valuable between them. Whisper into your hands, "I am placing my editor here for the moment." Take that editor and put it somewhere safe, but away from you; under your chair, or up on a shelf. Put it somewhere you can go back to, but that won't bother you for now.

For now, I just want you to read these brainstormed lists; soak yourself in the abundant rainfall of ideas. Don't think about why they might not work for you or what hasn't worked in the past. Yes, some of them cost money, and some cost time. Yes, some of these might be logistically difficult. However, figuring that piece out happens in step two. That step will also take creativity and resourcefulness, both qualities that can get stronger—like a muscle the more you exercise it. This is excellent exercise. Don't criticize yet. Your job for the next few pages is to stay open to elephants.

My parents have always supported my interests to the best of their abilities.

When I was young, I was extremely interested in dolls. My parents always supported that and would buy me the Barbies I wanted when they could.

This might sound superficial to some, but for me it was everything! I wanted to have my own doll line when I was older, and more importantly, I wanted to open a "doll museum" where I would one day put my entire doll collection and other dolls as well for people to view and see the history of dolls over time, and as a result, the history of fashion and technology along with them.

This was a huge passion of mine for years, and my parents were extremely supportive and would always encourage me to pursue what I loved - an attitude which has continued today, with their immense support of my various passions including make-up, video games, film, and much more.

I know I can always share my interests with them.

— JAYN

~

The Brainstorm

There are a lot of places to get more specific ideas for supporting your kid's interests. Some of my favorites are good-old-fashioned Google, Pinterest, and Instagram. I've found there to be a few common interests that tend to worry parents, so I want to start there. Your child might share one of these interests which will make this an easy place for you to start too. Or, read through and see if any might apply to what your kid is currently into.

Sometimes, I've included how one thing can connect to another and then another, and so on—similar to one of the earlier exercises. It's a fun game to play, even if your kid doesn't follow anywhere close to the same connected path. I've also shared some other considerations when applicable, like intriguing food options or field trip ideas.

One more thing. We often come to an interest with preconceived notions or biases. It is my intent for you to look at your actual, real-life child and their actual, real-life interests with fresh, glowing, loving, expansive, curious, kind, and playful eyes. With that in mind, I've also included characteristics or traits they might learn, values that might be embodied, and interest-specific benefits they might accrue. This is an exercise in reframing your potential biases, and actively looking for the green grass on *your* side of the fence.

And remember to use your journal to add your own connections, places to go, or things to look up for any interest.

BRAINSTORMED LISTS

Computer/Console Games

Games like *Minecraft, Fortnite, Overwatch, Super Smash Bros.*

Benefits

Strategic thinking, critical thinking skills, physics, mathematical thinking, teamwork, spatial reasoning, leadership, work ethic, perseverance, creativity, communication, eye-hand coordination, reaction speed, analysis, self-esteem, mastery, leadership.

Food

Think easy to eat at a computer, bite-sized, not sticky. Carrots, celery with peanut butter, trail mix. String cheese cut into cubes with toothpicks. Nuts, sliced fruit.

Possibilities

- Check out YouTube videos for Minecraft servers, making your own server, making their own YouTube videos.
- E-Sports, event management, sponsorships, tournaments.
- Game design, marketing, research benefits, debate among psychology professionals, JaneMcGonigal.com, sexism in video games, diversity representation in video games, console design, controller design, museum of technology, future of VR and AR, character design and different skins, costume design, cosplay,
- Communication methods and technology, how community forms, cultural change.

Little Figure Toys

Toys like Shopkins, L.O.L. Surprise! Dolls, and Hatchimals.

Benefits

Imagination, creativity, problem solving, nurturing, categorical thinking, storytelling, interpersonal intelligence, communication, leadership.

Possibilities

- Collect them all!
- Check out collection lists online, and different generations of collectibles.
- Display cases, carry cases.
- Does your child have what they need to display and catalogue their collection?
- Photography and taking photos of their collection.
- Trading groups.
- Hide figures in Easter eggs, freeze in ice, hide in Play Doh.
- Storytelling, stop-motion animation, writing scripts.

YouTube Unboxing Videos

Benefits

Interpersonal awareness, exploration, market research, relaxation, curiosity, storytelling.

Possibilities

- Make your own.
- How do people make money with YouTube?
- How much money do people make?
- Demographics of YouTube stars or families.
- YouTube conventions, marketing, play, different types of toys, toy design, recording equipment.

Rough-and-Tumble Physical Play

Benefits

Cardiovascular benefits, muscular benefits, longevity, physics, spatial reasoning, eye hand coordination, gross motor skills, risk assessment, self-esteem, confidence, leadership.

Possibilities

- Martial arts, trampoline places, laser tag, gymnastics.
- Finding every variation of tag there is, find a pool.
- Crepe paper to simulate lasers in a hallway and climb through, the floor is lava, obstacle courses, drag a hose to a playground, massive amounts of Oobleck, jump rope and Skip-Its.
- Hiking and big play on fields, adventure playgrounds.

Make-up, Hair Color, and Body Mods

Benefits

Imagination, aesthetic development, creativity, visual ability, design and spatial reasoning, ability to project and predict, problem solving, self-esteem, confidence.

Possibilities

- Get thee to a beauty supply store!
- Color hair with henna, chalk, Kool-Aid.
- Nail gels and stickers.
- Halloween stores, movie and television makeup, special effects, Disney jobs.
- Mannequin head, Play-Doh doll hair.

Candy, Ice Cream, and Sweet Treats

Benefits

Cultural awareness, science, chemistry, nurturing.

Possibilities

- International snack subscription boxes, ice cream museum.
- Field trips to candy stores, behind the scenes tours.
- Books and movies like *Charlie and the Chocolate Factory* and *Chocolate Fever*, make your own ice cream in jars or plastic baggies, make rock candy.
- Pop Rocks are fun all on their own, Mentos in Coke, jelly bean taste test, Jelly Belly factory tour.

Toy Weapons Play

Benefits

Teamwork, leadership, strategic thinking, eye-hand coordination, fine motor skills, concentration, aim, logical thinking, spatial reasoning.

Possibilities

- Nerf guns.
- Ancient history, world history, current events, filmmaking, fight choreography, making weapons, LARPing.
- Designing on Minecraft or other games.
- Paintball, laser tag, BB guns, shooting, hunting, leadership skills, battle tactics.
- Fantasy books and movies, war museums, history of toys made in factories, plastic and construction, safety gear.

Tabletop Games

Benefits

Strategic thinking, critical thinking skills, physics, mathematical thinking, teamwork, spatial reasoning, imagination, conflict management, taking turns, patience, perseverance.

Possibilities

- Check out the "Geek & Sundry" YouTube channel and International Table Top Day in April.
- Libraries often have game playing days and clubs.
- Many local game stores have drop in days, or specific game days scheduled.
- Lots of games at conventions like Comic Con.

- Subscription boxes, check new games out of the library, get game apps on your phone.
- Create your own rules and see what happens.
- Create your own games.

Phone Games

Benefits

Relaxation, stress reduction, ambient sociability, connecting with family, palette cleansing, feeling of satisfaction, distraction, escapism, eye-hand coordination, fine motor skills, staying current in pop culture.

Possibilities

- Make an app, phone contracts, why some apps are only available on iPhones.
- Game design, why some have great replay value, how to make money through games, advertising effectiveness, color theory, feedback, theory of flow, history of phones, museum of technology.

Princess and Fairy Tale Play

Benefits

Leadership, self-esteem, creativity, storytelling, self-expression, communication, learning morals, right and wrong.

Possibilities

- Theater, movies like *Into the Woods*, fairy tale retellings, every culture's *Cinderella*.

- Children's book illustrations, book fairs and expos, Disneyland, Lego sets, Star Wars movies, Medieval Times, Robin Hood.
- Magic, witches, history, allure of villains.
- Psychology, discussion of wealth, power, responsibility, history, geography, cultural differences and roles.
- Dresses and symbols, crowns and gemstones.

Disney (and other specific brands)

Benefits

Storytelling, heritage connection, history, moral development, connection to others, knowledge bank, sense of mastery, creativity, expression.

Possibilities

- Disneyland, Disney World, international theme parks, theme parks in general.
- Theme park video games, hidden Mickeys, Imagineers, Disney TV shows, studio tours.
- Toy collectibles, cartooning, history of animation.
- Superheroes, Star Wars.
- Building a ride, physics and science, how many visitors attend theme parks daily, what's the process of creating a new show.
- Feminism and princess movies.
- Copyright laws, famous voice actors, composers.
- Urban legends about Disneyland, Disney gangs, pin trading.

Watching Netflix

Benefits

Connections to other cultures, pop culture, recreation, relaxation, knowledge, engagement, learning new things, cultural anthropology, palette cleansing, amusement, enjoyment, family time, connection to others.

Possibilities

- What shows are they watching? Find more that are similar.
- Get the IMDb app and learn about the actors, directors, and writers.
- How a TV show gets made: the process, experience needed.
- Where they film. Is there anything filming nearby?
- Costume designers.
- Historical accuracy.
- Lighting design, sound, music.
- Cinematography.
- The history of the camera.
- Different kinds of film and how they look.
- How different genres of movies and TV are portrayed.
- Favorite food to snack on for different shows.
- Themes.
- Marketing.
- Measuring success.
- How streaming has changed ratings.
- Metrics. Reasons for cancelling a show.
- Rules for streaming on different services.
- Funding sources.
- Advertisers.

- Competition.
- Target audiences for different streaming services.
- What is a monopoly?
- Economics.
- Why do you like to watch that show over and over again?
- New discoveries.
- What makes a show familiar and comforting?
- Story arcs, character development, pacing and structure.
- Third acts and what makes a compelling story.

Knitting, Crocheting, Fiber Arts

Benefits

Fine motor skills, math notation, mathematical thinking, cultural awareness, history, connection to past generations, decreased stress and blood pressure, cardiovascular health, memory and attentiveness, perseverance, problem-solving.

Possibilities

- YouTube videos, crochet groups and knitting guilds, yarn stores, county fairs.
- Yarn bombing and needle felting.
- How to dye yarn with Kool-Aid.
- 4H clubs, subscription boxes, selling on Etsy.
- Heritage arts, fiber arts around the world, animal husbandry, natural versus synthetic fibers.
- Social justice and fiber arts, ageism and fiber arts, economics and fiber arts.
- Fiber arts connect to everything, seriously.

Cooking

Benefits

Creativity, expression, problem-solving, nurturing, interpersonal intelligence, cultural awareness, science, chemistry, fractions.

Possibilities

- Watch reality TV cooking shows, record your own.
- Fun gadgets like pasta rollers and egg timers.
- Picnics in unusual places.
- Chemical reactions of different foods.
- Go to restaurant supply stores, behind-the-scenes field trips to restaurants.
- Cook, play with food coloring in food, get food delivery service boxes.

Cosplay

Benefits

Creativity, sewing skills, imagination, small motor skills, hand eye coordination, interpersonal communication, expression, teamwork, self-confidence, public speaking, photography, event management.

Possibilities

- Conventions, theater.
- Sewing and DIY tutorials.
- Specific characters, their universe and origins.
- Comic books, movies, video games.
- Cool places to get costume pieces like vintage stores or thrift stores.

- Special effects makeup, contests.
- Renaissance fairs and other costume-wearing events.

Make Believe Play

Benefits

Imagination, creativity, problem-solving, therapeutic benefits, interpersonal awareness, emotional intelligence.

Possibilities

- Theater, dance, performing, puppetry, Shakespeare, musicals, television, animation.
- Storytelling, creative writing.
- NaNoWriMo.
- Cosplay, comic books, science fiction, movies.

THIS IS ONLY THE BEGINNING

Y ou made it! Along the way I hope you have had many sweet, funny, and playful moments with your children. I hope you realized a few things about your past and noticed some small successes and their giant impact.

I want to remind you that this is only the beginning. I used my experience with families to try to anticipate the questions and the exploration needed for many people, but without knowing you, this book can only be a starting point. Find a therapist, bring them this book and the answers you have written in the pages. Explore your story even more thoroughly. You and your family will be better for it.

We have discussed why it matters, we've explored what happens when it goes right and when it goes wrong, and you have many questions to keep pondering as you observe your children. Your actual, real-life children right there with you.

Here's one final takeaway. Maybe write these out and put them in your wallet or on your mirror so that you see them often until they become a habit.

Ten statements to show your support of your kids' interests

I'm impressed by your dedication.
I have noticed how focused you are.
I love watching you do that.
I am so interested in this!
That looks totally fascinating.
That looks like it took a lot of work to get there.
You've really become an expert.
This reminds me of something I loved as a kid.
I'll be right back; I'm just getting snacks.
I can't wait to see more.

Ten questions to show your support of your kids' interests

Can I see?
Will you show me how you did that?
Where did you learn how to do that so well?
What is your favorite part?
What is the hardest part for you?
Can I show off a photo of that to my friends?
Can you help me learn?
Do you have advice for a beginner?
Do you want me to help clean up?
Can I bring you any food?

SELECTED BIBLIOGRAPHY

Chapman, Gary, *The 5 Love Languages: The Secret to Love that Lasts*, Chicago: Northfield Publishing, 2014.

Brown, Stuart, *Play: How it Shapes the Brain, Opens the Imagination, and Invigorates the Soul*, Avery, 2010.

Gray, Peter, *Free to Learn: Why Unleashing the Instinct to Play Will Make Our Children Happier, More Self-Reliant, and Better Students for Life*, Basic Books, 2015

Loucks, Shannon, *Love More: 50+ ways to build joy into childhood*, Forever Curious Press, 2019

McGonigal, Jane, *Reality is Broken: Why Games Make Us Better and How They Can Change the World*, Penguin, 2011.

McGonigal, Jane, *SuperBetter: The Power of Living Gamefully*, Penguin, 2016

Nims, John Frederick, "Love Poem" from *Selected Poems by John F. Nims*, Chicago: University of Chicago Press, 1982. Reprinted by permission.

Numeroff, Laura, *If You Give a Pig a Pancake*, New York: HarperCollins, 1998

Russell, Ruth, *Pastimes: The Context of Contemporary Leisure*, Brown & Benchmark, 1995.

ACKNOWLEDGEMENTS

Thank you to Kiera for being my Executive Functioning, to Pam and Cyrus for being the child-raising pioneers that you are, to Daisy, Wyatt, Lilyanne, and Elinor for being the best teachers I could have, and to my ultimate partner in play and parenting, my husband Adam. Thank you all for your help, support, lessons, and love.

ABOUT THE AUTHOR

Roya has an M.S. in Counseling and a B.A. in Recreation and Leisure Studies. Roya brings play with purpose to several platforms. She is a Licensed Marriage and Family Therapist (#95302), with a private practice in Southern California and long-distance counseling for homeschoolers. Roya works with businesses of all sizes to help improve teamwork and communication, and is a professor of play at California State University, Long Beach. She believes strongly in the importance and power of play for all ages and continues to inspire others to become more playful. Her website is royadedeaux.com.

Roya specializes in therapeutic art techniques and has spent most of her life crocheting, knitting, making journals, collaging, and following other artistic pursuits. She gets to keep playing with clay and crochet through her handmade jewelry business, *Royaboya Handmade*, found at royaboya.com.

facebook.com/RoyaDedeauxMFT

instagram.com/royadedeaux

STAY IN TOUCH

Visit Roya's website, royadedeaux.com, to join her mailing list and receive updates by email about upcoming events, links to podcasts and publications, and information she shares around her favorite topics: play, well-being, and mental health.

Made in the USA
Monee, IL
28 September 2021

78970659R00120